T0208845

Witness of Change

Witness of Change

8 WEEKS OF DISCOVERY ON THE ST. JAMES'S WAY

STEPHANIE LEMEROND

authorHOUSE®

AuthorHouse™
1663 Liberty Drive
Bloomington, IN 47403
www.authorhouse.com
Phone: 1 (800) 839-8640

Published by AuthorHouse 11/15/2016

ISBN: 978-1-5049-0240-3 (sc)
ISBN: 978-1-5049-0239-7 (e)

Library of Congress Control Number: 2015904694

Print information available on the last page.

This book is printed on acid-free paper.

SANTIAGO

A Mother, A Daughter… A Pilgrimage
8 Weeks of Discovery on The St. James's Way

Stephanie Lemerond

Dedication

To Alain, my inspiring uncle

"In view of our fast-approaching departure, I faithfully train two or three times per week on random trails. During my first training, in the heat of July, I stumble over a medal type key-chain, featuring the number 18 in its center. 18 resonates in every French mind as the number to call in case of emergency. I pick it up, slide it in my pocket, thinking this will be my good-luck charm on the Santiago adventure.

A sign, without a doubt!"

—Alain

Contents

Author's Note

The Power of Change

While writing the account of my journey to Santiago de Compostela, one concept became dominant: The idea of change. Much of the story exposes change; from the total transformation a modern pilgrim must undergo to reach Santiago, the stunning historical changes that took place on the pilgrim's trail since the Middle Ages, as well as changes in people's lives or their perception of life that initiated their journey. And of course, there are the changes in culture and scenery that one encounters while ambling across 1,000 miles.

In life, change can be frightening, but also extremely powerful. In fact, a lot of success stories are built on change. Most individuals see their surroundings with minimal observational effort, missing out on the rich tapestry of detail that encircles them.

Being aware of our surroundings, such as noticing a person's expression that betrays their intentions or the tint of the sky announcing an approaching storm, makes us more assertive and apt to tackle the challenges we face.

This book will inspire you to embrace change and model this life experience to anything you want to accomplish, whether within your family relationships, your career, or your personal health.

Prologue

It all started one Christmas Day in Chatou, a little French town in the western suburb of Paris. A town located on a loop of the river Seine, home to the Impressionist Island, where artist Pierre-Auguste Renoir said, "You won't regret your journey; it's the prettiest location in the area surrounding Paris." My husband and I, my two children—age five and six at the time—and last but not least, our ninety-pound Irish Setter, were spending the holidays in Europe with my French relatives.

If you have never spent the holidays in Paris, you are missing out. In late November, Paris starts transforming into a winter wonderland. The capital ushers in the holiday season with considerable grace, its boulevards and districts lined with Christmas trees and Christmas decorations. The department stores set up their elaborate holiday window displays and the cheerful atmosphere is complemented with bright illuminations of the buildings, monuments and palaces.

Besides the Christmas tree, my parents' house is starting to resemble an American home. The many decorative pieces collected in the United States during visits have added a touch of American flavor to the more subtle French Christmas atmosphere.

The Christmas spirit infuses the house, with decorations, French Christmas music and a five-course meal to share. The house, large and open, is full. Grandparents, uncles, aunts, kids and dogs are keeping us busy and cheerful. As I tend to the guests, I overhear my mother, Michele, and her brother, Alain, in the middle of a serious conversation. They are looking over detailed maps and conferring about hiking.

Now, hiking is a significant subject to my heart. It is a topic that takes me back to my young years growing up in France. I hiked one Sunday every month since I was six years old with a group of family and friends. So many memories and smiles come to my face as I recall these days, shine or rain, and all seasons including snowy winters. We would hike on trails averaging eighteen miles with our backpacks loaded with tasty French supplies. Try to picture French hikers with French taste buds—hikes would not be the same without perfect cuisine. It did not matter how heavy it was; what mattered was that we looked forward to a very gourmet lunch. And we would not lower our standards just because we were hiking.

We would always meet at the church parking lot of a village early in the morning—for the French that means 7 a.m. Then we would head for the bakery to buy our fresh baguettes for sandwiches as well as croissants and *pains au chocolat* to start the day. Stepping in the shop, the buttery, sweet aroma would surround us and open our appetites big enough to buy half the store. Our morning would be interrupted by a mid-morning snack of: *Rillettes,* a goose, duck or pork meat spread, *saucisson* and *pâté* in crispy baguette sandwiches, camembert cheese and more.

But the main meal would be our gourmet lunch. First we had to find the perfect spot, with a view and enough space for all to sit. We would empty all backpacks and start gathering our supplies. Often we would barbecue and grill lamb chops and sausages, after appetizers, and typically enjoy a good bottle of red wine followed by coffee to end a flawless meal. A little nap was valued by all who wished. We would resume with much lighter backpacks and walk all afternoon, some regretting their excess consumption. As you might have already noticed, French people talk a lot about food.

Figure 1: The scallop shell (seen here fastened to the backpack) is the symbol carried by pilgrims throughout their pilgrimage.

Since hiking is a very dear subject to me, I jumped in to see what my mother and uncle were considering when I heard them discuss the tentative plan of a hike. My uncle was always the outdoor guy, in charge of orchestrating all the details of the hikes.

Parisians are very fortunate to have access to miles and miles of trails available to hikers. Trails cross small villages, farms, ploughed fields, forests and meadows, and follow country roads. They are very quiet and generally well-marked. This time, Alain had a different type of map and an out-of-the-ordinary guide book which triggered my interest even more. Amused by my puzzled face, they finally shared their project with me. My uncle had been working on this for a while, looking at options, researching all modalities and finally exposing his findings to his sister. They told me they were planning on walking, one week at a time, to *Saint Jacques de Compostelle* as we say in French, the famous St. James's Way. It sounded so amazing! Thus, when my uncle suggested I join them, I did not know how to react. Part of me was thrilled at the thought of participating in such an adventure, while the other part was trying not to overreact to avoid a potential big disappointment later. At this time, I had two children and lived 4,000 miles away from France in the American Midwest. The thought of asking my husband about this yearly trip sounded plainly unreal.

But how could I stop thinking about this amazing, once-in-a-lifetime opportunity? Filled with adventure and challenge, I could not. We finished our vacation and returned home in time for school.

I approached my husband with all of the best arguments I could think of, and to my surprise, he agreed to it. I was so excited. From that point on, planning became key. Reading books and guides, looking for advice, gathering gear and tracing road maps was electrifying. We were about to embark on a major adventure, a dream come true.

Introduction

But what is the St. James's Way in the first place anyway? It is a series of trails that begin in multiple locations across Western Europe, all ending at the cathedral in *Santiago de Compostela* in northwestern Spain, where the relics of St. James are buried. Medieval pilgrims came from Spain, Portugal, France, England, Germany, Switzerland, and Central Europe.

Just as one can easily depict a modern hiker with his backpack, poncho, and comfortable hiking boots, the medieval pilgrim had a typical look, too, characterized by a wide hat, leather sandals, and the *bourdon*, a thick stick.

What makes this pilgrimage route unique, compared to the routes to Rome and Jerusalem, is the profound imprint it has left on the landscape. Step by step, hour by hour, the modern pilgrim can witness the transformations that took place all over the European territory. Monuments, monasteries and churches, built to help, guide and encourage the medieval pilgrims, highlight the routes to Santiago over hundreds of miles.

The St. James's Way has attracted many in recent years, from hikers eager to tread the footsteps of medieval pilgrims while empathizing with the austerity of that era, to those who wish to refine their relationship with God. There are many reasons that motivate people to become pilgrims in this day and age, but it is noticeable how many undertake this pilgrimage at a turning point in their lives. They find help through a time away from their crisis, while dealing with the hardship of a route which prompts reflection and promotes healing. In a nutshell, a diversity of backgrounds, nationalities, and reasons populate the trail.

Let's take a quick look back at religious history. James and his brother, John the Evangelist, were called by Jesus as they were working with their father as fishermen in the Sea of Galilee. James first preached in Judea and Samaria, and then went to Spain to sow the word of God. When he saw that his work was unavailing, he took some disciples back to Judea and started preaching there again. Over time, the Jews became angry with him and brought him in front of Herod Agrippa to condemn him to be beheaded. According to the tradition, after the apostle's death, his disciples placed his body in a boat and embarked with him to escape the Jews. Trusting the providence of God and the help of angels, they drifted away and reached the shores of Galicia in the western region of Spain. The saint is believed to have been buried there with the two disciples.

Figure 2: The Cathedral of Santiago - Plaza Obradoiro

Year One

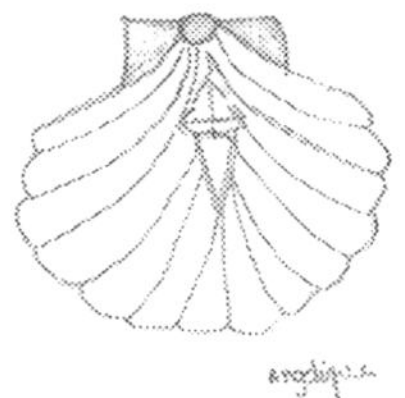

From Le Puy-en-Velay to Estaing
97 miles in 5.5 days

"*The heart of man plans his way, but the Lord establishes his steps.*"
-Proverbs 16:9

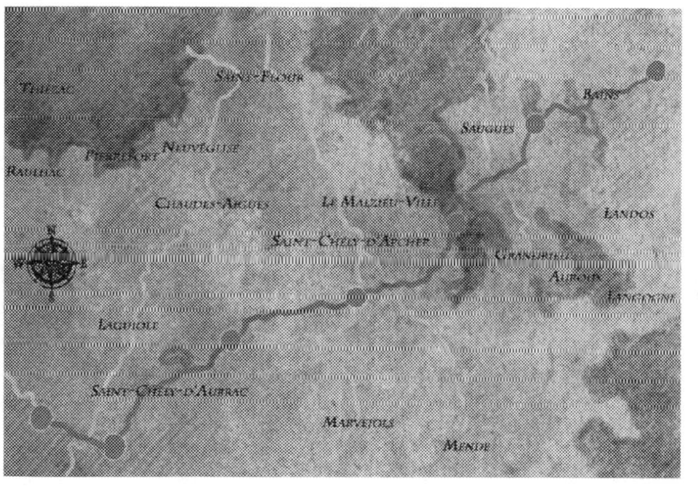

This is it! I can't believe it! I am all in one piece, nothing stood in the way; I did not even break a leg. Owning horses and being involved in hunter and jumper activities, it has been in my mind to be extra careful these last few weeks. You never know what can happen with horses. Today is Wednesday and I am flying out tomorrow from Green Bay, Wisconsin, to Detroit, and then straight to Paris. My uncle, mother and I are scheduled to leave for the center of France early Saturday morning. I will land in Paris on Friday morning—France is seven hours ahead of Wisconsin—and have a day to recover and adjust to the jet lag. It will be perfect.

My mother calls me, as expected, to finalize last-minute details. To my disbelief, the tone of her voice is not jolly as I pictured it would be, but rather muffled with uncertainty and heartache.

"Alain had a heart attack this morning," she ventures. "He is at the hospital. He is safe now, but he is staying at the hospital for more testing."

I am shocked. My heart is racing. I don't know what to think or say. She voices her thoughts of cancelling the whole trip and we hang up. This is undeniably unexpected. Who could have suspected such a tragedy?

We both go on with our mornings, thinking, and I call her back with the fruit of my reflection. Risking to be labeled insensitive, I have decided that nonetheless I will travel to Paris, leaving tomorrow. My airplane ticket is bought and I am not going to let it go to waste.

"Mom, I don't think that Alain is going to be able to walk on the trail for some time," I spill out. "And with that in mind, I think we should go and do this together, you and me. I know he will understand."

And without a definite answer, I hang up and prepare for my trip.

I catch my flight the next day and arrive in Paris the following morning as planned. My mother and I drive to the hospital to visit with my uncle. He still is in intensive care, but out of danger, and we are able to talk to him. After a while, not without apprehension, we expose to him our idea to go on with the pilgrimage and hit the trails without him. His face, torn between disappointment and understanding, is heartbreaking. Sensing the room filling with regrets and disillusionment, we awkwardly promise to call him every day to report on our advancement. This poignant scene remains imprinted in our minds as we drive silently back, wondering if we are making the right choice.

Back at the house, we work on final details, emptying and repacking our backpacks a few times, comparing and adjusting the placement of each item. Our bags are weighed, including water and food. We have all the gear recommended to be successful: Hiking clothes, change for the evening, sleepwear, rest shoes, toiletries, sleeping silky sheet called *sac à viande* in

French, and of course all kinds of pharmacy and first aid items. Ready to be a snail for a week!

Saturday morning, we get up at 5:30 a.m. and leave shortly after, bright and early. We have a six-hour drive from Paris to *Aumont-Aubrac*, the halfway point of our hike, where we have decided to park the car. We follow the highway to the south and drive with the rain for a good hour, stopping a couple of times for croissants and tea. Caught in our deep conversation over Alain and this regrettable situation, we almost run out of gas as we near *Clermont Ferrant*, with only a two-mile range left in the tank.

The *Viaduc de Garabit*, a majestic and colossal one-way railroad bridge, built by the Eiffel Group, pulls us out of our depressing mode, and such man-made beauty cheers us up.

Arriving in Aumont-Aubrac in time for lunch, we look for a traditional restaurant, wanting to immerse ourselves right away in the local culture. The restaurant Prouhèze en Gévaudan offers just that.

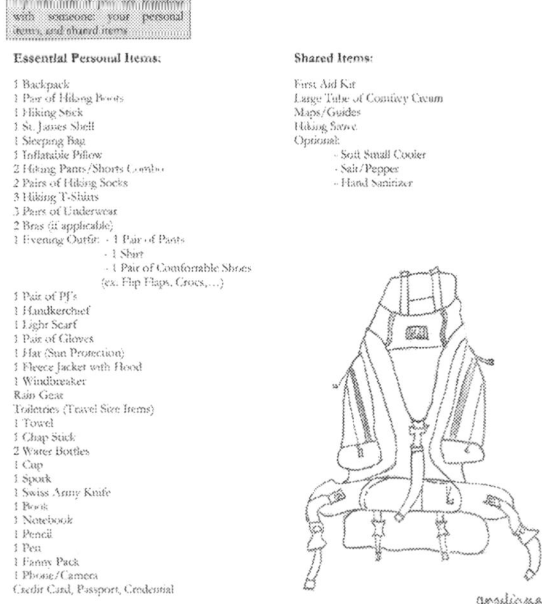

PACKING LIST

As a snail carries his house around,
your backpack carries all your essentials.

A Friend, a Need and, a Pest at Times!

The content can be split into two [illegible] with someone: your personal items, and shared items

Essential Personal Items:

1 Backpack
1 Pair of Hiking Boots
1 Hiking Stick
1 St. James Shell
1 Sleeping Bag
1 Inflatable Pillow
2 Hiking Pants/Shorts Combo
2 Pairs of Hiking Socks
3 Hiking T-Shirts
3 Pairs of Underwear
2 Bras (if applicable)
1 Evening Outfit: - 1 Pair of Pants
- 1 Shirt
- 1 Pair of Comfortable Shoes
(ex. Flip Flaps, Crocs,…)
1 Pair of PJ's
1 Handkerchief
1 Light Scarf
1 Pair of Gloves
1 Hat (Sun Protection)
1 Fleece Jacket with Hood
1 Windbreaker
Rain Gear
Toiletries (Travel Size Items)
1 Towel
1 Chap Stick
2 Water Bottles
1 Cup
1 Spork
1 Swiss Army Knife
1 Book
1 Notebook
1 Pencil
1 Pen
1 Fanny Pack
1 Phone/Camera
Credit Card, Passport, Credential

Shared Items:

First Aid Kit
Large Tube of Comfrey Cream
Maps/Guides
Hiking Stove
Optional:
- Soft Small Cooler
- Salt/Pepper
- Hand Sanitizer

After lunch, a scheduled taxi takes us to Le Puy-en-Velay, our starting point. We listen to our driver promote the attractiveness of his region during the hour-and-a-half drive through the countryside, arriving midafternoon at our hotel in Le Puy. We embark on a visit of this mystic town, the commencement of the pilgrimage in the medieval times for many pilgrims.

Starting our tour with the ascension of the mount Corneille to see Notre Dame de France, we warm up our calves for tomorrow. The statue of Notre Dame de France, the Virgin Mary, looms over the town atop a 2,500-foot hill of volcanic rock. Constructed in iron and painted pink, the statue was made from melted-down Russian cannons given to the town by Napoleon III after they were captured by the French during the Crimean War. We reach the statue's feet to witness one of the most spectacular sights in the region.

"My feet are burning," I complain while descending the many climbed steps. "I bet I have a blister about to erupt.

"Darn! Right before we leave tomorrow!" my mom adds.

A touristy shop at the bottom of the steps features pilgrimage paraphernalia where we buy our *bourdon*, the traditional walking stick used by the medieval pilgrims. Equipped with a metal tip, it served as a defensive tool against wild and aggressive animals, and also helped in muddy and slippery terrain. To keep track of time as if leaving the civilized world, we decide to carve a mark for each day we hike.

Walking through the old town, we stop at a small shop turned into a pilgrim welcome venue. It is a place to meet other pilgrims, ready to start their adventure the next day as well. A kir, a glass of white wine with a dash of red currant liquor, is graciously offered to us while we discuss and get to know each other.

Today is Saturday and we fear that only a few stores will be open tomorrow Sunday. So at 8 p.m., we enter a local supermarket, 8 à 8, and find some provisions for our lunch tomorrow: Ham, cheese, fruits, chocolate for quick energy, cookies and bread. Our dinner at the Kanter Brau Restaurant, including fresh oysters, *petit salé* and lentils from the Puy, known for its famous lentils, ends a full day. Closing our eyes after 10 p.m., we fall asleep setting mental scenes of what tomorrow might look like.

*****

"Good morning!" says my mom in a singing voice. The excitement is at its peak along with a little apprehension. We get up at 6 a.m., and after a quick shower and a light breakfast, we head for the cathedral for the weekly 7 a.m. Sunday Mass dedicated to the pilgrims, eager to start their new adventure.

A great mass perched on a volcanic hillock, Notre Dame is a complex, impressive and unusual monument that dominates le Puy-en-Velay. From the old lower town, a steeply inclined street leads us up to a monumental staircase of sixty steps which, in its distinctive, unique manner, reaches the facade, striped in white sandstone and black volcanic rock.

About twenty pilgrims are attending Mass, waiting to be blessed before they start their journey. After Mass, the benediction is granted to all present in front of the statue of St. James and the Dame du Puy. We are invited to grab a handwritten prayer to carry on our journey. My prayer is a word of encouragement from a seasoned pilgrim who is now on his way to Jerusalem. Before being sent on our way, we receive a medal of the black virgin from the priest to protect us on our voyage. In the sacristy, our credentials are stamped by a nun as proof of our departing the city. The credential, also referred to as a passport, is an official document that we need to carry throughout the pilgrimage to show the route we chose to walk to Santiago. Many places on the way, sleeping facilities, churches, and even restaurants will have personalized stamps that we will look forward to have on our credential with the date of passage, always impatient to discover the stamp they left on our roadmap. The design of the stamp is unique to each place, some being very creative and representative of the trail while others are boring and insignificant.

Bonne route à St Jacques. Maintenant
je pars à Jérusalem. Prions pour la
Paix. Prions pour l'Europe. Prions pour
que Dieu ouvre nos coeurs à l'Amour,
au Dieu qui Est de nos frères et soeurs
juifs, au Dieu bienveillant de nos frères et
soeurs musulmans, à Notre Père plein de
tendresse et de miséricorde de nous tous,
frères et soeurs chrétiens. Que Dieu vous bénisse.

Figure 3: Prayer Translation:

Have a safe journey to Santiago! Now I am leaving for Jerusalem. Let's pray for peace. Let's pray for Europe. Let's pray for God to open our hearts to love, to the God who is the God of our Jewish brothers and sisters, to the benevolent God of our Muslim brothers and sisters, to our Father, filled with tenderness and mercy for us all, Christian brothers and sisters. May God bless you.

Back at the hotel, we grab our backpacks and head to the beginning of the trail, Place du Plot. It is already 9 a.m. and we have a lot of miles to cover today.

Right away we learn this undertaking is not going to be a promenade. The little road used to exit Le Puy climbs non-stop and is a killer. The weather is beautiful, sunny and warm, but hot for this first climbing day. We discover blisters shortly after our departure. Our soft skin, not accustomed to this treatment, is wondering what crazy project we signed up for.

We take a break in Saint Christophe for a *menthe à l'eau*—a refreshing glass of mint diluted in cool water—in a bar and resume our climb to Montbonnet to reach 4,265 feet, a 2,132-foot climb from Le Puy. A couple of miles before Montbonnet, we find an open field and decide to take a break for lunch early afternoon.

The terrain keeps on climbing and shortly after lunch, the rain starts. We are in the forest, surrounded by mountainous terrain, and the steady rain turns into a storm, with lightning, hail, and thunder echoing in the mountains, bouncing from one hill to the other. The downpour is so sudden that the rain is gushing down the rocky trails. The trails are transformed into muddy torrents, which make it hard to walk and see where to put our feet. Our rain gear is keeping us dry, but it is cumbersome. With our hoods snuggled tight over our heads, we can barely hear each other. Walking one behind the other, our legs spread out to walk on the raised edges of the trail; we can't see one another.

Figure 4: Signage in France - GR 65

"Do you know if we are on the right path," shouts my mom to overcome the noise of my hood rubbing back and forth on my ears, between two thunder rolls.

"I'm not sure; I have not seen a mark for a while," I shout back.

The marks we refer to are red and white, two-inch-long stripes painted on tree trunks, rocks, fences, electrical poles, road signs, walls or anything that is available that guide hikers and pilgrims on their journey. But beware; if you happen to see a red and white cross, you missed your turn. You must turn around and start looking for the right path.

Heads bent down, we look at our feet, stepping here or there, avoiding slippery rocks and uneven ground. Did we miss a sign, a turn?

"Hang on; I think I see something white on that tree over there!" I shout. Getting closer, I clearly recognize the waited-for, priceless and little reassuring sign. "We are on the right trail," I confirm.

"How long before the next village?" she asks.

"I'm not sure exactly, but based on the time, we should reach one soon," I reply.

My mother, uneasy about storms in general, is forced to push forward hoping that the next village is near. A few hours earlier, our backpacks had felt so incredibly heavy on this first day, dealing with the heat and the interminable hills. But now, caught in this tormented weather, our minds focused on the potential danger, we find extra energy and forgetting our load, feel as light as can be.

We finally arrive in St. Privat d'Allier, a lovely little village in the mountains around 4:00 in the afternoon and are yet unsure of the next step to take. It is still early, but the weather is very disruptive. To our surprise, we run into a group of pilgrims who also started this morning from Le Puy en Velay, whom we met last night at the welcoming get-together. They are having a drink in a little café, trying to dry off a bit, waiting for us and starting to wonder where we were, considering the weather conditions we are facing.

Even though the rain continues to pour, the thunder has stopped. Feeling much safer in the company of our new friends, Luc and Jean-Philippe from Bordeaux, and Robin and Hilary from Vancouver, we bravely walk another hour and a half and arrive in Monistrol-d'Allier, our planned stop for the night. We have a reservation in a hotel, *l'hôtel des Gorges*, while the others are staying at the *gîte*; so we split upon arrival and walk our own ways.

The hotel, closing the very next day for the season, is very rustic but dry. You can hear the flick-flock sound coming from our shoes filled with water as we walk in the lobby. After a long, hot shower, we stuff our shoes with newspaper, a hiker's trick we had read about to soak up the moisture, and hope for dry shoes the next morning.

"Allo Alain," says my mom as her brother picks up the phone in Paris from his hospital bed. "What a day! Wet and tired, we were happy to arrive at the hotel. With the storm roaring above our heads all afternoon, we almost stopped early, if it was not for a group of fellow hikers who babysat us for the last four and a half miles."

As her voice fades away, I dose off on my bed waiting for dinner.

In the dining room, a few tired-looking pilgrims are already seated for dinner, recovering as well from their first harsh wet day. A couple from Switzerland, a man alone wearing shorts, a t-shirt and flip flops, and us, quickly engage in a lively conversation reminiscing the events of the day. With red and hot cheeks, colored by the fresh air and red wine, we leave the dining room, head back upstairs and sink deeply into our beds. Looking back at this first day, we replay each and every detail in our minds as we drift off to sleep.

*****

We casually wake up at 7 a.m. and depart soon after for a new episode. As we leave Monistrol, we also leave the Velay region to enter the Gevaudan. The terrain is hilly and challenging through a lush countryside. We make our way toward Saugues, where we are able to stock up with food for lunch at a *charcuterie*. In fact, we have walked all morning without seeing a place to buy anything to eat. This raises a red flag that we need to keep track of where and when we can stock up for each day.

A statue on the heights of Saugues welcomes the visitors and reminds us of a scary legend. Back in the eighteenth century, two regions, Aubrac and the Margeride, were infested with wolves. One of the wolves came out of the nearby forests in the vicinity of Saugues. In July 1764, a child disappeared. Picking his victims among humans rather than among the flocks, the wolf created a real panic wave among farmers. He was described as having a strange tawny fur, possibly covered with scales, as tall as a donkey, with shorter legs in front and endowed with enormous claws. During three years, the *Bête du Gévaudan* would have—according to the legend—massacred about one hundred women and children. It isn't until June 1767 that Jean Chastel kills the beast, in the northwest of Saugues, and puts an end to the massacres.

Figure 5: My mother, Michelle

We leave Saugues and make a stop a couple of miles further in a pine forest to enjoy a well-deserved lunch and a mid-day rest. Even though we can't help thinking about the killing beast of the legend living in the nearby forest, the scenery is peaceful with sunrays filtering through the trees, lighting up a secret square where tree trunks entangled on the ground make a perfect seating.

The afternoon is a little long, and when we finally have our next stop called Le Sauvage in sight, we are thrilled as much as exhausted after this twenty-mile hiking day. The last two miles seem endless, progressing on a sinuous trail, inching toward Le Sauvage, just a pencil sketch away in the distance. A massive farm house with interconnected outbuildings sieges on a vast clearing, suffused with evening pale light and surrounded by a dense, dark forest.

Upon arrival, we visit the farm store that sells a few farm-made products and buy bread, ham and cheese to contribute to the shared dinner with the same group of friends we met last night. Combining all of our supplies, we dine on a wild mushroom omelet, picked during the day, ham and cheese, and pasta. A few glasses of wine and lots of laughter seal the beginning of a week long friendship on trail GR 65.

The group is expanding and now encompasses: Luc and Jean-Philippe, the *Bordelais* friends, Hilary and Robin, the married Canadian couple, Philippe, the loner we met last night at the hotel, and my mother and me, labeled as the mother-daughter tandem.

The site is memorable as described in books, and we pass a fantastic evening cooking and eating in great company by the fireplace. We spend our first night in a mixed dormitory with the group –a new experience that undeniably implies pros and cons. For us newcomers, mixed feelings float in our mind; the convivial sense of community, being part of a personable group, sharing jokes and stories. Laughing conflicts with adjusting to practical necessities like changing, organizing and washing personal female clothing, sharing bathrooms and such. It is a step into a new world we have yet to discover.

*****

As you can imagine, the beauty of sleeping all together in a dormitory is that when the first pilgrim decides to get up and get moving, the whole dorm is forced to follow. So, against our will, we get up at 6:30 a.m. and have a hearty, countryside breakfast made of toasted country bread, cheese and tea. Departing at dawn, our breath hanging in the chilly air reminds us of the coming season, when nights are cold, but days are still warm. We carefully follow the signage to avoid getting lost.

After crossing departments from Haute Loire to Lozère, we hike in a group formation, changing partners every so often, to arrive later on at St. Alban-sur-Limagnole. (Departments in France are political entities similar to states in the US.) We take over the whole terrace of a café adjacent to a Roman church, distinguished by its bell wall so typical to the region, with three embrasures each occupied by bells.

We are now in a region called La Margeride, a mountainous area situated in the *Massif Central*, known to be a world aside, where inhabitants have learned to tame the vast deserts. The farms are massive and the granitic traditional houses appear to be part of the surrounding decor. The vast spaces we follow, suitable for the herds to migrate to the grazing grounds for the summer in the highlands of the Margeride, resonate with a tradition that started way back in the Middle Ages. The Transhumance is the migration from lowlands, where the animals spend the winter, to mountains, where pastures become available during the summer. In late spring, the Aubrac cattle get ready to go up to the high pastures, where they will remain until mid-October when they return to their lowland stables. On the day of Saint Urbain—a Sunday at the end of May—a great, colorful transhumance festival with herds of thousands of cows, harnessed with flowers and heavy bells takes place.

Our supplies for lunch today are: mackerels marinated in white wine, ham, olives, cheese, bread and *framboisine*, a regional raspberry pastry. We walk for another couple of hours and make a group stop for lunch under the trees.

"Who wants coffee?" offers Luc, while assembling his attire to brew trail coffee.

Tempted by the hot beverage, I gladly indulge on a cup of the black French treat. During the afternoon, we little by little spread out as everyone, dealing with their own troubles, is eager to arrive and not so patient to walk at somebody else's pace. Only two and a half hours to go and lots of *Coullemelle* mushrooms to pick on the way. Among the tall grass in the bordering fields, we can spot white hats reaching up on long, delicate stems, waiting to be picked. In view of a tasty dinner, we attach plastic bags to the back of our backpacks, and meticulously fill them up with the precious harvest. We arrive late afternoon and settle in the *Gite du Berri* in Aumont Aubrac. The first ones arrived have already selected and reserved a dormitory for the group; a little room with bunk beds accommodates seven people, with private toilet and shower.

We are now becoming more and more organized, and after deciding on a menu, we split up and head for the different stores in search of ingredients for our feast. We start with a mandatory aperitif: *Pastis*, olives, sausages and nuts, followed by a main course of: beef steaks, mushrooms, sautéed potatoes, salad, cheese, dessert and wine. A typical invigorating five-course meal!

After being disconnected from the world for two days, we are finally able to make phone calls to our families. It is a comical sight to see everyone hanging on a cell phone talking to a loved one somewhere in the world. Did medieval pilgrims have this luxury? Was bringing reassuring news to their loved ones left behind an option? They were gone for months with very little or no means of communication. Something unheard of in our modern world! A world in which we feel better if our children carry a cell phone with them while attending their after-school activities.

Our feet have been taking a beating the last two days. Blisters have turned into bloody-looking wounds. It is painful, ugly and scary. The risk of infection is not negligible, so it is a must to take the time to disinfect the open wounds every night. A daily ritual is implemented following Luc's protocol, which consists of injecting a red substance with a syringe into the wound to clean and prevent infection. Our feet are a real source of discomfort, especially the first fifteen minutes that follow any break during the day. It starts with an excruciating pain, which eventually fades away as the foot becomes numb to it.

Today ends on a nice note; everyone is tired and sore, but all in good spirits. Our dorm is cozy to say the least, although confined and stacked up would be a more accurate description. Every inch seems to be occupied by something or someone. But all in all, friendship is greater than room size. Our "leader" Luc, always jovial, exuding an air of well-being, decides to become the massage therapist for the night. It is delightful to lie down and have a relaxing foot massage before bed. Community life does have pros after all.

*****

It is already Wednesday and hard to believe. Time is going by fast, and every day each one of us is getting more attached to each other. We leave Aumont with the sunrise after a morning routine which is gradually taking place. Chaze de Peyre, one of the first villages on our route this morning, is a small village with typical vaulted houses covered with slate roofs called *lauzes*.

The group is striding forward together following the Roman via of Agrippa until we reach the café Chez Régine, where we must stop to warm up and have a bite to eat. Our fingers feel ltike they are frozen, but any minor reasons are always taken into consideration to make a stop, set down our backpacks and enjoy a warm café, hot chocolate or tea, with fresh croissants.

Figure 6: L'Aubrac Plateau

Our next step is a favorite of all times: the beginning of the plateau of Aubrac, with an elevation averaging 3,937 feet, but culminating to 4,920 feet high. Officially leaving the Margeride, remembered for its soft slopes, we come upon a new land, L'Aubrac, distinguished by interminable pastureland. The stunning deserted landscape is awe-inspiring and conveys a sense of freedom to those who look at the immensity lying at their feet. The area is characterized by a volcanic and granitic plateau, whose last volcanic eruptions date back to 6 million years ago.

Bovine breeding is the main activity on the plateau, and it has its own bovine species called Aubrac, which is well-adapted to this environment. The pasture, demarcated by stony walls built in bygone days, is inhabited by bovines, totaling up to 50,000 head roaming on the plateau. This small cow is so unique that one cannot help taking pictures of her unique face. She has a honey-colored coat, and her eyes are lined with black eyeliner, or so it seems. Not shy, she likes to come and pose for pictures over the uneven, rocky walls.

The trails on the plateau are majestic and prone to contemplation. Everyone walks in single file and savors this moment of serenity, alone in this grandiose environment, where the eye searching for an attraction finds only the quiet horizon and the mind wanders as it pleases.

We arrive at *La Croix de Ferluc* and decide that in this specific location, we need to remember and celebrate our first milestone. Right in this place, we have hiked the first 100 kilometers of our journey, a memorable number to be proud of. So as good French fellows, we drink to our accomplishment with a sip of red wine, excited to be together.

As the day wears on, we continue to stride the paths on the plateau and unexpectedly find a lady perched on top of a rocky pasture wall.

"Hello, could you give me a hand to help me get down?" she asks with her biggest smile.

Climbing up there to take pictures, she had been unable to get down and was waiting for a charming rescuer to appear. We set her free and set out to look for an adequate spot to settle for lunch. While searching, we encounter a family, also on their way to Santiago, with two donkeys. Indeed, the trail can officially be accomplished by foot, bike, horse or donkey. Traveling by donkey is a little less predictable than using your own feet. Donkeys can be stubborn and slow the pace down quite a bit. However, there is little to carry as the donkey is glad to carry the load for you. This appealing option is only a dream while we pass them and comprehend that our shoulders only will carry our personal items.

In Nasbinals, our next evening stop, the group settles in a *gite communal*, where we are able to secure a room for eight. The lodging is comfortable, clean and spacious in comparison to last night. Our early arrival in the middle of the afternoon gives us plenty of free time to spend on regular tasks such as showering, journaling, grocery shopping and socializing. The family with the two donkeys arrives later and ends up staying in the same shelter.

In the kitchen, a young couple, hikers as well, but carrying backpacks weighing fifty-five pounds, invites us to sample a glass of Absinthe from Andorra. Absinthe was the drink of choice among artists and writers in the mid- to late nineteenth century. In the cafés of Paris, the cocktail hour became known as *l'Heure Verte*, the Green Hour. Absinthe was considered a vivifying elixir long before it could be ordered in a cafe. Ancient absinthe was different from the liquor that Verlaine and Picasso imbibed, generally being wormwood leaves soaked in wine or spirits. As its popularity grew, so did public hysteria over its mysterious effects and drunkenness. Absinthe was the subject of many studies into alcoholism; at the time it was referred to as Absinthism. Its use was even considered a one-way ticket to the insane asylum. Commercial production ended around 1914, but can now once again be purchased according to a safe and legalized recipe.

Tonight, we are not cooking; we are going out, the whole group. What a sight! A group of this size, loud, tired and dressed in *fancy* evening clothes, proceeds to invade the one village restaurant, eager to sample local dishes. The waiter advises the most popular meal made of sausage and *Aligot*, a traditional recipe from the Aubrac region. The rich, thick and sticky starch, named Aligot, is a mixture of homemade mashed potatoes, butter, sour cream, garlic and a cow cheese called *Tomme*. This meal, definitely satisfying and filling, is just what we needed after a long outdoor hiking day.

Aligot

Serves 6

Ingredients:

- 3 lbs medium potatoes, peeled and quartered
- 8 garlic cloves, peeled and finely chopped
- 1 glass dry white wine
- 4 oz unsalted butter
- 1 oz plain flour
- 4 tbsp. crème fraîche/heavy cream
- 1 lb Tomme/Gruyère/Raclette or Cheddar cheese
- salt and freshly ground black pepper

Method:

Boil the potatoes in salted water until tender. Turn off the heat, drain, then return them to the hot pan to dry out for five minutes. Mash.

Gently sweat the garlic in a little olive oil until translucent, then pour in the wine and turn up the heat. Allow to reduce until there is hardly any liquid left in the pan.

Reduce the heat and melt in the butter.

Stir in the flour and allow to 'cook-out' for a minute.

Add the mashed potato, crème fraîche and cheese, then stir over a medium heat until well combined.
Continue to cook until the mixture bubbles, then season with plenty of salt and pepper.
Serve with farmers sausages.

*****

It has already been five days of living the dream on the Camino trail. Time is flying and we are starting to anticipate the end of the week. This adventure can be hard and even painful at times, but so fulfilling and fascinating at other times. It is a constant battle with ourselves, whether our mind is whining on the purpose of this journey or our body complaining from aches and wounds. But the reward is so gratifying that we just keep going.

Hilary, the Canadian lady, has forgotten her hiking stick this morning in the lodging. She decides to walk back to the town and get it. All of us take a break and wait for her return. It is a short wait, since Hilary is so tall and has super long legs, to the despair of my mother and I, who are much shorter. In fact, it is at times frustrating when I walk next to her in an even and straight path, sharing thoughts and comparing American, Canadian and French lifestyles, to notice that while she is casually making one step, I have to take two to keep up with her rhythm. Unfair, plain unfair!

This morning, the weather is mild; the landscape is astounding as we are still walking in the pasture on the plateau, heading toward Aubrac, a once known and important stop for pilgrims back in the Middle Ages.

Unfortunately for me, the beauty surrounding us is not appreciated to its just value. I am starting to think the Aligot I enjoyed so much last night is starting to disagree with me. One hour and a half to go before the next hamlet, hoping that something will be open. Needles in my stomach, heavy backpack, and trails wrapping themselves on the hills and descents is making this morning less charming than anticipated.

In the meantime, we have to decide which route to follow; we have options. One way is more marked than the other, but a little longer. The other is, according to the books, a little more adventurous, offering fewer markings.

Nevertheless, there is no fog around at the moment, so since the weather is in our favor, we certainly have few chances to get lost.

We are reaching the highest point of the plateau, crossing pastures among herds of cows, or at least we hope there are no bulls. We make sure to carefully close the wire gates for every one we have to open, each time entering a field where loose herds are enjoying their mornings. The cows and sheep are just looking at us go by in our funny costumes and deformed shapes. We imagine them laughing at us for the grotesque sounds we make to catch their attention.

My stomach, quite opinionated at the moment, reminds me of the urgent need to find a bathroom ASAP. The hamlet is now in sight. We arrive and find a hotel restaurant opened. What a relief! So while everyone is resting, enjoying a nice hot beverage in the bar, I take over the bathroom with great pleasure and expect to be done and over with this debilitating trouble.

We resume our momentum toward St. Chély d'Aubrac, where we conveniently buy groceries for lunch. Another urgent stop is required at a café across from the store. Relieved, but tired, I am ready for a real break.

Shortly after, always in search of the perfect spot to picnic, we find a farm court opened, protected from the wind, deserted by the inhabitants, probably on vacation at the moment. We settle in and pass around *patés*, hams and cheeses, fresh bread, wine and more goodies to replenish the used up energy. We respectfully make sure to leave the area as clean as we found it, noticing a sign kindly written offering hospitality, but stating the garden is neither a garbage nor a toilet. Imagine this. Your home is located on the trail where thousands of people walk by every year. Would you keep your yard open to passersby or fence it all for privacy?

Only six miles to go this afternoon to reach St. Côme d'Olt, the agreed halt for the night. The afternoon drags and plodding along, we arrive close to 6 o'clock. Our afternoon was interrupted a few times with different collections along the way. We found walnuts on the trees but ready to eat, grapes in the fields, apples and figs. What a delight! There is nothing like eating your snack from the tree itself.

Figure 7: Hiking Late Afternoon

Figure 8: Grabbing a Snack

We have now entered a new department called Aveyron. Our lodging is located in the center of the village, in an old building inside of the old fortified walls of the village. As usual, we get cleaned up and tend to the necessities first, and then start looking for a café where we can relax.

The town is particularly cute and goes back at least to the eleventh century, when the Roman church was built. There is, however, a unique and noticeable church tower with a helicoidally shape.

Tonight's dinner takes place in a large, long, old-fashioned kitchen heated by a large fireplace. Laughter, red cheeks from the fresh air and red wine, make this last night an indelible scene, except for one sad incident. Only six of us are sharing a room tonight. One is missing in the group. Jean-Philippe, one of the fellows from Bordeaux, had to stop his adventure today, forced to abandon due to a nasty infection. A couple of days ago, Jean-Philippe developed an extensive blister on the ball of his right foot. He was uneasy to admit that he was in pain and thought that all would get better quickly. But when you walk about twenty miles a day, six days in a row, your feet are your best friends and you ought to treat them with the greatest respect. He, unfortunately, did not allocate enough of his attention to caring for his hurt foot. The blister turned into a bleeding wound, and shortly after that, he woke up with a swollen foot and soon came down with a general infection. Lack of care and his hiking trip was over.

How sad and disappointing for him and also for his hiking companion Luc. We said our goodbyes to Jean-Philippe, wishing him a quick and painless recovery, leaving him in good hands at a nearby convent with attentive sisters.

*****

Today is Friday, our last day. Everybody's favorite morning music goes off from our cell phone and announces it is time to rise and get moving. Six-thirty seems a little early, but necessary to ensure that everyone is ready to roll at a reasonable starting time, usually around 7:30. We have now accepted that showers are only at night, then so appreciated, on top of being essential after a sweaty and even cruddy day. There is simply no time in the morning to savor a shower. Indulgence is only allowed at night, sort of like a well-deserved reward, while mornings are focused on basic necessities.

Three miles to reach Espalion brings us there mid-morning while the local outdoor market is going on. What an entertaining scene, where appetizing smells and colorful displays reveal the French secret of farmer's markets. We split for a while, take a hot chocolate and bathroom break in a café, while others roam through the little town.

The time has come for us to call our taxi, who we decide will meet us at 2 p.m. in front of the church of Estaing, a village located seven miles away. The group starts moving again, but being the last and final stretch, everyone seems to be walking at a slow stride. The terrain is a little challenging and we make many mini-stops over nothing important, just feeling the end near.

But now it is getting close to our meeting time and we have to hurry to our destination. The goal is to share a last lunch all together before we board our taxi. We arrive at the doorway of the village, a bridge crossing the Lot River. The village is hanging from the other slope of the valley. We pause here to wait for the tail of the group, sitting on the wall overlooking the river.

Two priorities are on the agenda. A bathroom break is imperative, since we are going to have a good hour and a half ride in our taxi to reach our car in Aumont Aubrac, and we need to have our credential stamped from this last stage halt. We find a hotel in the main street which fulfills both needs.

We now move toward the church, centrally located as always in French villages. Luc settles on a stony wall adjacent to the church and proceed to open his backpack to unveil an unsuspected surprise. To celebrate our departure and embrace our friendship, he wanted something special for our last meal together. To our great amazement, he has bought a roasted chicken at the market in Espalion and carried it all the way here. Filled with emotions, rushing through our minds and touched by such a sweet thought, we inhale this delightful lunch while the taxi parked at the end of the alley awaits us. The bells are ringing; it is now officially 2:00 in the afternoon, time to say our goodbyes. Such a sad moment, we want to push back some rushing tears. With the help of the whole crew, we load our backpacks and hiking sticks in the trunk and proceed to kiss everyone as French people do, warmly on the cheeks. Time to hop in and wave goodbye from behind the rear window. This is an image that is engraved in my memory: this group of friends waving at us, on a little church place in the countryside of France.

After a weeklong excursion of adventures, laughter, pain, feasts, sharing bedrooms and bathrooms, supporting each other morally on hard days, spending hours disserting on private matters and world issues, it is saddening to leave. Plus, we realize that while we must go home, they are moving on together on their way to discover new trails, new adventures, without us.

In Aumont Aubrac, we find the garage that has been keeping our car for the week. We grab some lunch and make a last stop at the cooperative where they are selling local cheeses. Time to hit the road to return to Paris. Six hours during which we go over every single details, laugh at situations that happened, and review everyone's personality.

One week, 100 miles, we are hooked! One week away from the modern world, one week reconciled with basic human needs, we are hooked! One week, during which priorities have changed, during which the meaning of eating, sleeping, and drinking have changed. We are hooked! One week, during which we have learned the power of talking or being silent. We are hooked!

One year to wait! One year to prepare! One year to share with friends and family! What will next year bring? New adventures, new encounters, new dishes, new scenery!

Year Two

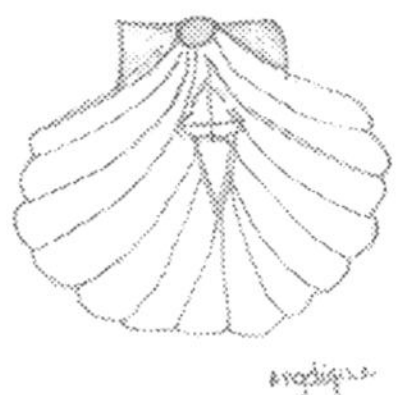

From Estaing to Cahors
108 miles in 6.5 days

"Blessed is the man who remains steadfast under trial, for when he has stood the test he will receive the crown of life, which God has promised to those who love him."
James 1:12

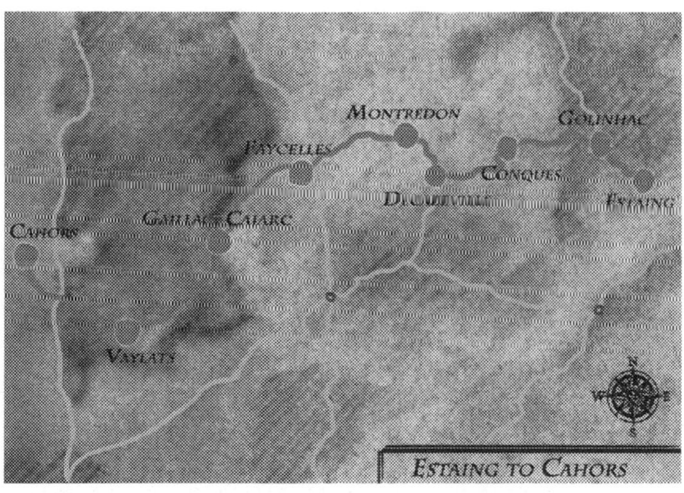

On the third week of September, as the leaves are starting to turn colors, we faithfully resume our pilgrimage started a year ago. Our mind is full of vivid memories from last year. This time, the two of us only, dedicated to our long-term commitment to go all the way to Galicia, return to where we left off last September.

I arrive from the US on Thursday morning, all prepared and eager to get started. After visiting with my dad and grandma, my mom and I undertake to go over our backpacks, item by item, following our made-up list. Twenty-two pounds without any food.

This time, we board a morning train at *Gare d'Austerlitz* in Paris, which takes us to Brive La Gaillarde a town in the center of France. There, we board a one-car-long train heading for Rodez. Our stop is Decazeville, where our reserved taxi is waiting. Our taxi ride, lasting about one hour, brings us back to Estaing, where we separated last year.

He drops us off at the bridge entrance, where the trail starts. No need to cross the Lot River to go into Estaing. We have ten miles to go and no time to waste as it is already 3:00 in the afternoon. In spite of the two and a half miles going uphill right from the get go and the rain, we reach our next stop, the town of Golinhac, in record time. Three and a half hours, while the guide we carry estimates four hours and thirty minutes are needed to cover this distance. It is damp and wet, but it does not matter. Nothing can stop us; we are loaded with energy and good spirit, ready to do this. The muscle memory is working; our body and our mind remember this sensation so vividly that we feel like we are swallowing the incoming trails. Our rhythm is magical.

We meet no one during three and a half hours through forests, fields and clearings. Only a golden retriever, who follows us for four miles all the way to the inn where we are staying. Upon arrival, the dog is welcomed in the back room, next to the kitchen, with a bowl of water, while the hotel owner makes calls to find the dog's owners. It is not long until Sir Dog gets a ride home in a private car. Our hotel, La Bastide d'Olt is tidy and cozy, and perfect for this first night. Our room, painted in spring grass green, is welcoming and relaxing. The window of our bedroom opens up on a watercolor painting of rolling hills where Aubrac cows are grazing. The mouthwatering aroma climbing the stairs to our room sparks our stomach to life and ushers us down to satisfy our palate. Dinner takes place downstairs in the large, rustic dining room, where massive country-style tables for twelve are there to share with other pilgrims.

The dining room is loud, filled with pilgrims eating with great appetite. We're glad to know we caught up with a busy stop point and won't be alone on the trails tomorrow. We join a table of French and French Canadian hikers and savor a duck leg *confit* to die for, washed down with a regional mild red wine.

*****

Our routine seems to fall back right into place as we get up at 7:00, enjoy a typical French breakfast and depart around 8:10 a.m., alone on the trail. We quickly pass hikers who had left in the early hours and walk toward Espeyrac and Senergues, known for its castle and church with a square tower.

There, we load up on supplies for lunch and cross the large forest of Senergues. At the top of a strenuous hill, we find the ideal place for lunch in the woods, overlooking beautiful scenery and making other hikers envious when they walk by. Forty-five minutes of idleness, sheltered from the wind. This was worth every effort. The scents, the sight and the peaceful, quiet environment, except for the metallic clicks from the hiking sticks of the few hikers that pass by, are priceless.

Figure 9: The Village of Conques

The afternoon goes by fast as we trek downhill on a steep, deeply embanked and stony trail. We arrive in Conques, a graceful tiny village, highly picturesque and tranquil, nestled at the bottom of a valley. The Saint Foy abbey-church, a magnificent Romanesque church, emerging from the center of the village, was a popular stop for medieval pilgrims on their way to Santiago. The main draw was the remains of a saint, a martyred young woman from the fourth century. The abbey-church stands in the middle of the village, dominating the landscape, but harmoniously so—its tall, pointed towers blending among the roofs of the medieval houses that huddle closely around it. The fortress-like facade overlooks a small, cobbled square and is surrounded by terraced gardens.

On the outside, the most notable feature of the otherwise plain church is a large Romanesque carving of the Last Judgment in the tympanum over the main doors. It was sculpted between 1107 and 1125 under Abbot Boniface. The scene is full of activity, expression and detail, and some of the original colored paint still remains. Pilgrims coming from Le Puy and Estaing entered Conques on rue Haute. Then in the abbey-church, pilgrims circled the shrine of Saint Foy three times before stopping in front of the golden reliquary-statue to ask the saint for a safe journey to Santiago, which might take them up to a year of dangerous travel. After visiting the shrine of Saint Foy and resting, the Santiago pilgrims moved on to Figeac and Cahors through the Porte de la Vinzelle.

We enjoy a well-deserved cold beer on a charming, sunny terrace garden, covered with greenery and overlooking the roofs of houses, before undertaking the visit of the village. We meander through the winding streets, taking in the imposing abbatial and the ancient monastery. Parts of the medieval walls still survive, along with three of its gates. The houses date from the late Middle Ages and are divided by cobbled lanes and stairways that are a pleasure to wander through.

Tonight we are staying in a small hotel, l'Auberge St. Jacques, a Logis de France, in the main street of the village, facing the abbatial, with a bathtub in the room. We chance on a shop selling soaps and spa items, and purchase a lavender relaxing bubble bath for immediate use.

As we keep browsing around in the village, we fall in love with a mini silver scallop seashell in the window of a jewelry store.

"Let's buy two, one for each of us," says my mom. "It will be a perfect addition to our medal from the cathedral in Le Puy. It will be 'the jewelry' of our journey."

This chain, displaying both symbols, will be the sole jewelry we wear every year during our pilgrimage.

For dinner, we settled for the pilgrim menu, a degustation of the southwest specialties of France; my favorites. A slice of *foie gras*, served with figs, duck *magret*, in other words the breast, cooked like a medium rare steak, accompanied with sauteed porcinis and the so feared Aligot, followed by a course of local cheeses. The dessert, an artistic creation served on a slate tile, exhibits creamy chocolate *crème brulée*, rhubarb compote, fresh fruit, and for the final touch, vanilla ice cream paired with a curved tile cookie, served on the lid of an old fashioned glass canning jar. A delight for the taste buds and for the eyes! And the best part is that with the miles we swallow all day long, we can swallow without guilty conscience all the tempting caloric desserts.

*****

Monday morning, we rise at 6:30 a.m., prepare our feet for a day-long hike, and go down to find the bar and restaurant still closed. We have to wait until 7:30 a.m. for the owner to get out of bed, bushy-haired, and serve us a frozen and microwaved breakfast, far from the quality of food we experienced the night before. Early and quality don't mingle well in this place.

We pay our dues and step out on the main street in the dark, asleep town. This morning it is damp and cold, and the paved streets are slippery from the storm that raged all night. The wet, uneven ground makes it hard to get a good rhythm going. We exit the village through La Porte de la Vinzelle, following the steps of thousands of medieval and modern pilgrims. Without a chance to warm up, we start the ascension of an unending hill, in the woods, for over thirty minutes to reach the St. Foy Chapel, rising to a point above the clouds. Our internal temperature has risen quite a bit. Hot and sweaty, we are tempted to undress, but the threatening sky convinces us not to.

While climbing, we encounter a Chinese young man from Paris, hiking and suffering. We suffer together for a while, sharing our sweat and effort, and split at the top of the hill when my mother and I make a necessary halt to celebrate our 125 miles, an even 200 kilometers. We have saved some wine from dinner last night in a plastic bottle for this special moment we knew was coming. This time we are celebrating alone, thinking about our first 100-kilometer mark celebrated last year with our hiking companions. We commit to maintain the started tradition, a wink to our friendship.

We pursue our route and by mid-morning find a stony wall bordering a working farm, where we make ourselves a cup of hot soup to keep warm. The clouds are menacing, and while we are in need of a break, it is hard to stay warm, so our stop is rather fast.

Figure 10: Practical Hiking Stove

Equipped with a convenient stove conceived for hikers, on which we can heat water to make hot soup and tea, we agree that despite the extra weight, this handy gadgetry is needed on this portion of the trail at this time of year when it is cold, wet and windy. Indeed the downfall is that this practical apparatus, containing an aluminum pot with a removable handle, a foldable three-side stand and a couple of gel substance starters, weighs about two pounds. This also implies that we carry dehydrated soup mix, extra water, tea bags and sugar cubes. But we opt for extra weight in exchange of extra comfort.

This morning is taking forever. We arrive in Decazeville at 1:45 p.m., the first town we crossed in three days. Disconnected from the real world, it is almost overwhelming. Cars are rushing to get back to work after their lunch break, and after being in the woods and small villages or hamlets for three days, we have lost track of this hectic world. Plus, we are exhausted after six hours of walking, arriving in this town too late to shop; all the food stores are now closed until midafternoon. Nowhere to stop, no extra energy to look for an out-of-the-way park or welcoming halt stop. We keep going, tired, hungry and still walking uphill. The hill is so steep, it seems our noses are touching the ground as we bend almost in a halfway position to ascend the hill and compensate for the weight of the backpack, looking for a place to sit down.

We reach the top of the hill and spot a grassy area on the heights of Decazeville, in a subdivision-type neighborhood, overlooking the valley and its town. We can now appreciate the view, noticing that this is an industrial region.

The commune was created in the nineteenth century because of the Industrial Revolution and was named after the Duke of Decazes, born in the late eighteenth century, Minister of Industry under Napoleon and founder of the factory that created the town. Originally called La Salle, the town is built on coal, which it has produced since the sixteenth century. It was exported in small quantities to Bordeaux by waterway on the Lot. The high point of iron production was reached early in the twentieth century, with 9,000 employees and one million tons of steel produced. The production then decreased, and the town has since diversified its industry: metallurgy, woodworking, metal fabrication, and production of steel tubing. Today only one open sky mine called La Decouverte is still around and can be visited.

Our lunch is frugal, munching on our leftovers; with only a piece of saucisson–a dry sausage specialty–cheese, and some chocolate. We are glad to be able to make a cup of tea. Not much to eat, but rest was most needed. The sun, finally here, is playing hide and seek behind a few large, low-altitude cottony white clouds.

We pack up and as we exit our mini field, we bump into three talkative men who we join for a while as we go uphill some more. We pursue our route to reach Livinhac le Haut one hour later. We meet again with the Lot River, which we cross before entering the village. This is our final stop for the day, a small village listed to have a restaurant, bar, lodging and a store. We find the café on the church place, get rid of our backpacks and sit at a table against the wall in full sun, enjoying a cool *panaché*, a beer mixed with Sprite, usually a quarter of soda to three quarters of beer. It is a drink much preferred by women in France.

As we come to rest in the sunny square, we notice that again all the stores are closed. It is Monday, and lots of retailers in small towns choose to close on Mondays to make up for their working Saturday and Sunday morning hours. So we are unable to buy food for tomorrow.

It is only 4:30 p.m. and there is not much to do in this town; no food to eat, no monument to visit, so we decide to push to the next village an hour and half away. Our shoulders and feet rested, we are ready to venture to Montredont.

The climbing terrain is more effort than we anticipated, and we are glad to see the steeple of the imposing grey church, announcing the village. The hamlet, elevated on a mount, overlooks green pastures and working farms as far as the horizon goes. We find a gite, La Mariotte, run by an amiable woman who welcomes us with a glass of homemade lemonade.

We leave our muddy hiking boots in an adjacent outdoor room and go upstairs to colonize our quarters, which is situated under the roof where the wood floor and wooden beams give out a warm, comforting feel. The main room downstairs, furnished with a long, family country-style table, a working fireplace, and a couple of inviting sofas is heartwarming after our long hiking day. A bunch of people, already in from their day, have gathered around the table in wait of dinner, deliciously homemade and local.

This nineteen-mile day has taken its toll on us and we are overly tired tonight. We have to keep an eye on our feet and backpacks, as they are sources of pain and trouble. Even though the memories from the first week on the trail were outstanding, one major hitch was darkening the painting: the agony prompted by our blistered, bloody feet. Hiking a week at a time has its advantages, such as time to find a solution to remedy the evil blistering associated with hiking. We could not possibly keep up at this rate. It would take us a mere week to go through the process of gaining blisters, healing and repairing before it was time to go home. Never a period long enough to make tough skin and be over the blistering issue. This could not happen over and over every year or it would become a dreadful nightmare!

Time was on our side to find a solution. Fortunately, a bright French pharmacist had an ingenuous idea for us. He suggested we buy a couple of rolls of Elastoplast bandages, about one inch wide to wrap our feet daily or as needed, on the heel of our feet and crossing back on the top of the foot to secure them in position. Following his advice, we were delighted to experience that thanks to its elasticity and adhesiveness, the band did remain in place for the most part, in spite of the up and down motion created while climbing or descending hilly terrain. The result was a major improvement compared to last year, but fine tuning was still necessary.

*****

Figure 11: St. James Stained Glass Window

On Tuesday morning, rested, we depart around 8 a.m., about half an hour after sunrise, and head toward St. Felix, home of the Roman church St. Radegonde. It is known for its tympanum from the eleventh century, representing Adam and Eve in front of the tree and the serpent. The colorful, worth-the-detour stained glass window of St. James holding his hiking stick attracts the hiker inside for a soothing intermission.

We meet hospitable locals throughout the morning, including an older man waving near his open well, a grandma looking ever so sad in a hamlet, another one picking mushrooms on the side of the trail, all eager to engage in conversation with us, as if in need of fresh news and company. These encounters give fuel to our imaginations, which willingly come up with all sorts of creative stories for these *characters* we don't know; creating their lives, the lives of their families and their villages, as we inhale the miles crossing this new region. What must it be like to live in such remote regions where the young have left for the larger cities, in search of work or modern lifestyle? Could we live like this, for more than a week, we ask each other.

This sort of seclusion can seem appealing at times, when we feel over-stimulated by our daily life. Back home, when the demanding world takes a toll on my own sanity, I picture myself reflecting on what it would be like to have a studio with large windows opening up onto the ocean or some other body of water. A place where I could create without distraction.

Don't we all need a personal haven? But all year round sounds a little too much for us raised in the city.

It is late morning by the time we reach St. Felix. We find a café and our mouths are watering thinking about the taste of a fresh croissant and a hot chocolate. The disappointment is huge when we are told there are no croissants or any other fresh pastries this morning. We inquire about a possible sandwich, no luck! What should we do?

Figure 12: Hearty Soup

After a moment, thinking, standing in the middle of the empty bar, my nose saves us. I can scent a beautiful aroma coming out of the kitchen behind the bar. Who does not ask, does not get, so I make my way to the kitchen door.

"What are you cooking back here? It smells wonderful," I inquire.

The cook, caught off guard, stumbles over his words a bit, and trying to get rid of us answers: "I am making a countryside cabbage soup for lunch, but it won't be ready for a while."

Picturing the hearty *potage* making its way to my starving stomach, I refuse to give up and beg for a bowl. Looking at my determined posture, the cook gives in and agrees to serve us.

We get all comfortable in the dining room area, still deserted, and wait for our promised bowls. Shortly after, our host comes out of the kitchen carrying a large tureen full of soup. He serves it with rustic thick slices of country bread, right in the bowl, soaking the flavorful juice. Our beaming faces thank him with large smiles. The aroma and the taste are so delightful that we both eat two large bowls of this regional cabbage recipe, full of vegetables.

Full and content, we are finally ready to move on and make our way to Figeac, our next stop, most likely where we will eat lunch. Food again! Indeed, food is a major drive in our daily routine; it implies eating, of course, but also a reason to put down the bags, take our shoes off and ease out.

Figeac is a medieval town in the Lot department of the Midi-Pyrenees, about forty-five miles east of Cahors on the Célé River. It has an extensive and interesting historical centre dating as far back as the ninth century. The old *colombage* houses, houses with first floor balconies, and narrow streets lined with ancient stone buildings and ornate carvings, form a lovely ensemble. Figeac was a welcome halt on the GR 65, a way also known as the "via podensis," one of the four major routes described from the twelfth century onward to reach the Spanish destination of Santiago.

Founded in 830 around a Benedictine abbey, the town became a prosperous centre in the thirteenth century, thanks to its strategic central position which encouraged agriculture and trade. The town expanded and the architecture reflects its growing prosperity. The four major mendicant orders known as Franciscans, White Friars, Dominicans and Augustinians established monasteries in Figeac, creating hospices, one of which became the pilgrims' hospice. To this day it houses the town's hospital—Hôpital Saint Jacques.

A mystery remains about two enigmatic monuments in Figeac known as les *aiguilles de Lissac* and *les aiguilles du Cingle.* Tall, octagonal columns of stone made of cemented, dressed stone, the constructions are placed on a pedestal comprising four steps. The needle situated to the south, le Cingle, measures about forty-seven feet while the Lissac needle, situated to the west of Figeac measures thirty-seven feet. No other constructions of this kind have been identified in France. Some, in Italy, have been dated to around 1300. They are said to have served several functions, such as beacons guiding travelers on the Way of St. James, but the reality of their purpose remains an enigma.

We arrive in Figeac with an after taste of disgust. We are exhausted, in pain, aching everywhere, and unhappy overall. It is 2 o'clock and we need to indulge. No picnic today, and forgetting that we are hikers for a moment, we find a restaurant with outdoor seating, in the sun, on the bank of the Célé River, next to a medieval bridge. This is just perfect to perk up our downhearted mood of the moment. We sit down and order a copious meal of veal liver, which turns out to be overcooked and basically terrible. We don't give up on the incident, determined to indulge at any cost, and order a glass of wine with cheese to end on a good note.

During lunch, we come to the conclusion that our backpacks are just too heavy. Some fellow men hikers had given us some advice back in Golinhac on Saturday. Stubborn and offended then, we now surely believe it. We simply cannot go on this way anymore. The decision is taken: we are in a larger town, and we will find the post office and proceed to eliminate as many items as possible and mail them back to Paris.

We leave the restaurant, locate the post office on the opposite bank, and on a bench just outside of the post office, we thoroughly inspect every pocket in our backpack, looking for any insignificant items and decide what is really necessary. We decide to share as many items as possible, get rid of items of comfort but not of necessity. Toiletries, extra clothes, reading book and other accessories that we can share are discarded. Looking at each item with regret, but associating an image of discomfort and frustration with it from this morning, we quickly lessen the hard task of disposing of any extravagant objects.

Before leaving town, we run into the group of new friends we met last night in Montredon. Figeac is their ending point, so we say our goodbyes and good luck.

This post office episode, lunch and a bit of conversation take up an hour and a half of our day. It is now 3:30 in the afternoon with at least another five miles to go, about two hours or more worth of hiking.

We arrive in Faycelles, a charming hamlet, at the end of a long, curvy countryside road. We have walked about ninety percent of the time on blacktop roads this afternoon and our feet are hurting; they feel numb and tingle from the hard and repetitive impact.

The landscape has changed through the day to be less broken and with softer hills. The vegetation itself is different, too. We were surrounded by a forest of chestnut trees, and now we are arriving in an area where walnut trees are everywhere, which is a good addition to our snacks. In fact, this afternoon we picked walnuts and figs that we plan on eating for dessert tonight after dinner, with a piece of *Camembert*, a French cheese, bought in Paris on Friday. The smell is now quite pronounced and indicates it is time to finish this fragrant cheese before all the hikers turn their head away as they pass us. We also spotted a lot of parasol mushrooms, but unfortunately they were inaccessible, out of reach behind the fences. What a shame! We can't help remembering the tasteful mushroom meals we prepared last year with the group.

Figure 13: Afternoon Tea Break

Throughout the day, we noticed little construction in the pastures, typical of the area, used as shelters by the shepherds. Looking like a little hut and made of white chalky stone, they are usually located near the trail on the side of the pasture.

For lodging tonight, we have found a very typical shelter. A couple of locals have restored an authentic *caselle*, the very same type of shelter we have seen all along. It has an adorable circular bedroom with apparent stones, and a bathroom built in an extension of the original caselle. Decorated in a tasteful manner, warm yellow tones connect the different elements of the room. We lay on our beds for a short rest looking at the unique construction and let our minds venture to an unknown world for us, the life of a shepherd.

There are no options for making dinner, but the hamlet is only 500 meters away with an open restaurant, according to our host. He assures us it will be easy to find even in the dark.

"You can't miss it," he says. "There is only one and it is next to the church."

We also learn there is a mini grocery store where we need to gather supplies for tomorrow. The village is newly restored and looks charming. We find the *La Forge* restaurant and relax over a local dinner with a bottle of wine from the Quercy region. The restaurant owner, also owner of the store, opens the store for us after dinner so we can buy picnic provisions.

The walk back to the caselle is rather interesting. It is pitch black and quiet, except for the countryside night sounds from nocturnal creatures echoing. All we have is a little electrical lamp to guide us, barely showing the road. Walking as fast as we can, tight against each other like two city girls, we make it safely back to shelter. Only after locking the door and feeling safe do we finish the evening, enjoying a feast of walnuts and "stinky" cheese.

*****

Today we allow ourselves a little later departure, since our planned stage is only sixteen miles. As we step out of our caselle, it is cold and fog is hanging over the countryside.

The morning is built around encounters of all sorts. During our morning break, sipping the usual hot soup, we are interrupted by a herd of sheep. The leader of the herd, ambling along his well-known trail, stops dead and holds up the whole group when he sees us sitting on the side of the path around a corner. The shepherd, not far behind, catches up to them and makes them kindly move forward with his knotty wooden stick. This older, talkative shepherd, from the village nearby, explains to us that the herd has been very protective this last few days.

Figure 14: Sheep Going to the Fields

"They are on the lookout for anything unusual since the baby was born three days ago," he says. Nestled among his peers, we notice him, adorable and already so alert! What a treat to witness nature in its fullness.

Speaking of animals, a garter snake is our next encounter this morning. Surprise! Enjoying the morning sun, he was stretched out on the rocky ground. The landscape is indeed changing again, getting stonier-looking to an almost deserted earth. In fact, except for the sheep and the snake, we see no one on the trail today and think to ourselves that it is a good thing to have each other on this adventure. We have seen a few ladies, young and older, alone on the Camino, and it is hard to believe when you think of the many stretches we are isolated in dark forests and remote trails. Sometimes, we do not see anyone for miles.

This new region, called Quercy, has a unique feel. It roughly runs from Figeac to Moissac and is known to be the ancient land of the Cadourques, a Celtic people present in the area during the Roman invasion. The trails are white for the most part and reflect a great luminosity, reminding us that we are nearing the south of France, known by artists for its unique light.

If you are fond of gourmet food, you may have heard of saffron. Worth twice the price of gold, saffron is a spice that comes from the pistils of the Crocus sativus. The aroma evokes the heat of the sun. It is used in Mediterranean cooking and surprisingly grows on the dry Quercy Causses, a limestone plateau. The saffron flower, which has a short life lasting about two days, emerges in October over a period of about three weeks. The saffron pickers repeat the same gestures their ancestors used in the fifteenth century. Each flower is cupped in the palm of the hand, the stem cut with the fingernails, a gesture repeated over and over again. It takes two hundred flowers to produce just one tiny gram of saffron. The pistils are removed and gently dried to produce "red gold" using an oven at 50°C (122°F), which dries the moisture and roasts the stigma, producing an intense aroma.

Along the way, we find a small cheese farm where we buy a fresh ewe's milk cheese, an ideal complement to our lunch.

Later in the day, we arrive in Cajarc via a narrow little trail, perched between a limestone cliff and a steep drop, a very popular stop for the pilgrims in the Middle Ages. A bridge was built on the Lot River in 1320 to ease access to the still-existent hospital built in 1269.

A small café on the main place is calling us with sweet words, so we make a stop there for refreshment. We then buy a few groceries for dinner along with a half bottle of Cahors wine.

Cahors is a red wine from grapes grown in or around the town of Cahors. The dominant grape is Malbec, which must comprise a minimum of 70 percent of the wine. It is complimented by 30 percent of Merlot and Tannat. Reflecting the traits of the Malbec grape, Cahors wines can be rather tannic when young and benefit from aging. Generally, Cahors wine is often similar to robust versions of Bordeaux wine.

During the Middle Ages, Cahors wine was called "the black wine of Lot." It was on the tables at the marriage of Eleanor of Aquitaine with Henry II of England. Pope John XXII, born in Cahors, made it his table and sacramental wine.

One hour to go to our final destination, a little hamlet called Gaillac. This late afternoon brings out a beautiful light shining on the corn fields. As we stand along the expansive fields, looking in the distance, I imagine the difficulty a painter like Van Gogh encountered when faced with a wide palette of tones like these golden shades ranging from yellow to flaxen to blonde, as he worked on his olive tree series in Saint-Rémy.

We make one last and unexpected stop near Gaillac, where we find a working farm selling strawberries; a perfect addition to our dinner menu.

Among strawberries, they also grow corn for the northern countries and tobacco, a specialty in the Lot for the last few generations.

We arrive in Gaillac and meet with Madame Lafon, who owns and rents a full-size apartment to travelers. She takes us through a little road between farm hay sheds and storage barns to a large shed. In the back somber corner, there is a wooden staircase climbing to a door, the apartment entrance.

The apartment is grandma-style from the 1960s, with checkered wallpaper, large flowered linens, worn-out gold carpet, and Formica kitchen counters. Nevertheless, spacious and clean, we like to believe, we settle in our flat for the night. The evening is very warm and we can enjoy the sunset while sipping a glass of wine on a large terrace overlooking the cultivated countryside.

At dark, we retreat in the kitchen-dining room area, where we turn on the TV to watch a movie while dining. Our evening is interrupted by an electrical shortage. The light goes off as we are eating. The room is pitch black, and unfamiliar with the apartment, we giggle at how helpless we are, hoping that someone will rescue us. Shortly after, we notice a ray of light shining through the kitchen window from the alley below. Someone equipped with a flashlight is coming our way. Monsieur Lafon is our saving knight, bringing candles for the night as according to him, this might happen again.

*****

This morning, we start with climbing a stiff hill to wake up our muscles in a foggy and cool countryside. We officially reach the Causse of Limogne, where it is advised to carry enough water, especially in summer. This enticing limestone plateau presents a diversity of landscapes alternating pubescent oaks, dry grasslands dotted here and there with junipers, and agricultural parcels surrounded by dry stone walls. By the time we arrive in the village of Limogne, the church bells are announcing lunch. Centrally located, a shaded small square with plane trees, a south of France icon, hosts outdoor seating for a couple of restaurants. The small menu laying on our table proposes tempting southern dishes. We fall for a fluffy porcini omelet with a glass of Cahors wine. Delicious!

The aroma emanating from the porcinis is to die for. Considered one of the safest wild mushrooms to pick, the flavor can be described as nutty and slightly meaty, with a smooth, creamy texture, and a distinctive aroma reminiscent of sourdough. Porcini are sold fresh in the markets in late summer and early autumn in central and southern France. Dried or canned at other times of the year, they are also distributed worldwide to countries where they are not found. They are eaten and enjoyed raw, sautéed with butter, or in pasta, soups, and many other dishes. In France, they are used in recipes such as *Cèpes à la Bordelaise*, *cèpe frits* and *cèpe aux tomates.* Porcini risotto is a famous traditional Italian autumn dish. Fully mature specimens can weigh about two pounds; however, the most appreciated by gourmet are the young small porcini, as the large ones often have worms and insects inside, and they become slimy and less tasty with age.

Porcini Omelet

Serves: 1

Ingredients:

- 1 large or 2 medium fresh porcini mushrooms
- 1 tsp. olive oil
- 3 eggs
- 1 tsp. water
- 1 tsp. butter
- salt and freshly ground black pepper
- 1 parsley sprig, chopped

Method :

Slice off the ends of the mushrooms and brush them gently. Using your fingers, gently remove half of the spongy bottom of the cap.

Slice the mushrooms in half lengthwise, and then cut the halves into 1/5 inch thick slices.

Heat the olive oil in a frying pan, add the mushrooms and parsley, and cook, stirring occasionally, until they start to brown and have given off and reabsorbed their juices. Remove from heat.

Crack the eggs into a bowl, add the water and whisk until frothy.

In a pan, heat the butter to sizzling and swirl it around to coat the bottom and sides. When the butter is starting to brown, add the eggs.

As soon as the eggs start to set, lift an edge of the omelet and tilt the pan to allow the liquid eggs to run beneath. Repeat several times, lifting different parts of the omelet.
Before the eggs have set completely, add the mushrooms and a tablespoon of crème fraiche. Sprinkle with salt and ground pepper.
Slip the omelet out of the pan and onto a plate, allowing it to fold over itself.
Serve with a green salad and French bread.

Our friends from Decazeville, the three gentlemen, are having lunch here, too. We are glad to see each other and recount everyone's last couple of days.

Three kilometers later, we make an obligatory stop in front of a Calvary to celebrate our 300 kilometers with a sip of red wine saved from our night in Gaillac, sticking to the tradition.

Forced to make a pause due to a crossing sheep herd, we discuss the region and our adventure with the shepherd. The bovines have changed into sheep; the oak forests are now dominant, which is a good environment for the growth of porcinis; the paths are very stony, with many crossing protected hunting lands.

The weather is beautiful again today, hot and sunny. As we traverse the little village of Bach, a thoughtful man calls us over to give us a handful of pears. Not suitable for selling due to their deformed shapes, he buys them to make *eau de vie,* a hard liquor. They are uneven, but very juicy. With juice running down our hands, we can taste how they have never traveled in trucks, but are just coming straight from the orchard, filled with sun.

After nineteen miles and a few stops, we reach Vaylats, known for its imposing convent, occupied for decades by the Congregation of the Daughters of Jesus. The sisters welcome only pilgrims on their way to Santiago carrying the pilgrim's passport.

Dinner is served at 6:45 p.m. sharp in the dining hall, with seventeen other pilgrims seated around two long tables, most of whom we have already met along the way. The nuns have already eaten, but they have cooked for us and are bringing out trays of food on carts. The food is basic but copious, meant to satisfy the voracious hikers.

In the pious edifice, the pilgrims bring a glimpse of the outside world with their loud, echoing voices, laughter and countless stories of what is happening on the trail. The evening is pleasant as we discuss, compare, and catch up. We have not seen some of these people for three or four days.

Our room for two is neat and tidy, with a view over the roofs of the convent on one side and the large park reserved for the nuns on the other.

*****

Breakfast is served at 7:00 a.m. sharp. Since nuns are serious about discipline, we make a point to arrive on time in the dining hall.

Yesterday, in order to come to Veylats, we had left the marked path for a detour of about seven hundred yards. We now need to return to it, and during the discussions last night at dinner, we found out there is a different route that would put us ahead on the trail instead of walking slightly back to where we came from. But no one seems to quite know where to find it.

One of the nuns jumps in the conversation and proceeds to indicate the correct route to follow, cautioning us that this route back to the common path is unmarked.

Once on the GR 65, we follow a Roman Via called the "Cami Ferrat" for about nine miles, a flat, long and monotonous portion, with little habitations and many oak trees.

For our morning break, we settle in a field behind a natural wall of trees and greenery, and proceed to warm up some water to infuse some tea. The field is ploughed, but offers a nice view and a quiet out-of-the way spot. An envious biker, a pilgrim on bike, drops by to share a cup of tea with us. This moment of spontaneity is what makes the trail so fun—people wanting to reach out, inquisitive about each other's origin, willing to open up and spend some time with others.

Later, for our last lunch of the week before heading back home for this year, we find a snug stretch on the heights of Cahors, about two miles away. We are prone to reflection over this week, comparing the dynamic of this year to last year's hike. It certainly is an emotional moment, again, though less dramatic than a year ago. The consensus is that it is hard to return to the real world, waiting for us, down there at the foot of the hills, with its demanding lifestyle.

Tucked into a rounded nook of the Lot River, Cahors is a lovely medieval city almost entirely surrounded by water. We arrive in Cahors through the Louis Philippe Bridge. On the opposite bank, a small office welcomes the arriving pilgrims with homemade lemonade and offers to stamp their credential.

Every day, each pilgrim is required to show proof of his route on his "pilgrim passport," also known as the "credential," with the stamp of a recognized entity. We personally decided to have our paper, a small cardboard booklet, stamped every night only where we sleep. A mistake as we learned upon the final arrival in Santiago is that a minimum of twice a day is required. Once in Santiago de Compostela, you hand in your completed credential to obtain the famous Compostela, the certificate proving you have walked the Camino de Santiago and completed your pilgrimage.

We have a little bit of time to visit the city before our train leaves for Paris. We find a café and after enjoying a drink, we beg the owner to keep our packs for a couple of hours while we tour the sites.

Figure 15: Pont Valentré, Cahors

At the heart of the wine country, the city, green and lively, is filled with history. The city's most memorable landmark is the Valentré Bridge and nearby ramparts. The fortified bridge is an example of the defense architecture of the Middle Ages. Also called the Devil's Bridge, this fourteenth-century structure is majestic with its three fortified towers and six arches.

The construction, which lasted over half a century, gave rise to the following legend: Exasperated by the slowness of the work, the contractor signed a contract with the Devil. Under the terms of the contract, Satan would contribute to the construction by sharing all of his savoir-faire. If he complies with all orders, the contractor would abandon his soul in exchange. The bridge rose quickly, the work was almost completed and the contract was coming to an end. To save his soul, because he did not want to end his days in hell, the contractor asked the devil to fetch water at the source of the Carthusians, for his workers, with a sieve. Satan returned, obviously empty-handed since the exercise was impossible, and lost his contract. Deciding to take revenge, the devil came every night to unseal the last stone of the central tower, known as the Devil's Tower, replaced the prior day by masons.

In 1879, during the restoration of the bridge, the architect Paul Gout set into the empty slot a carved stone with the effigy of the demon, who since then remains hopelessly hooked with its claws prisoner of the cement.

Leaving a part of our souls on the trail, we hop in our TGV fast train, out of Cahors at 6 p.m., which takes us straight to Paris Austerlitz and the end of this year's adventure.

Year Three

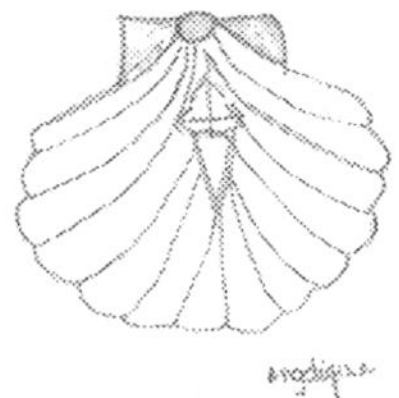

From Cahors to Nogaro
131 miles in 7 days

"Trust in the LORD with all your heart and lean not on your own understanding; in all your ways acknowledge him, and he will make your paths straight."
Proverbs 3:5-6

Friday morning, our train in Gare d'Austerlitz is waiting for us, ready to take us back to Cahors at high speed, where we left off last September, a short four-hour ride away.

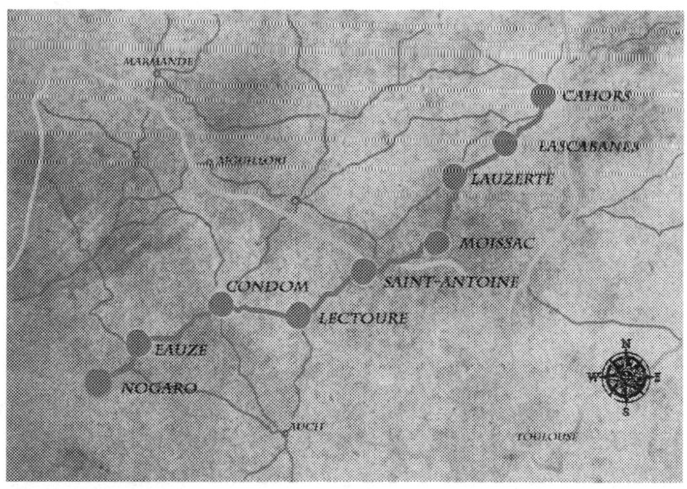

Figure 16: Le Pont Valentré, Cahors

Our arrival in Cahors is brutally uncomfortable, with a temperature of nearly 90 degrees F. Coming out of the cool air conditioning in the train, we load our backpacks on our back and set out to hit the trails. We start by crossing the Pont Valentré to go over the Lot River and attack the sharp ascent of a hill. The heat, lack of practice and terrain make it perilous. We take our time, as our veins are ready to pop out of our heads. I take off the lower legs of my pants halfway through the climb in an attempt to cool off. Out of breath, I constantly look back to check on my mother, fearing a cardiac incident. We endure this painful exercise, out of shape and melting in the sun, for about three miles. Even though we just started, we look at each other with bright red cheeks. We opt to stop for a ten-minute technical break on a nearby bench under a tree to undress, hydrate, and regain some energy with a chocolate bar.

Our next trail is situated on the crest of a mountain, where we stride for about four or five miles. Everyone is ahead; there is no one in sight. So we keep on moving before taking another ten-minute break. Three miles to go and we arrive in Lascabannes, our stop for the night. It is 6:45 p.m. and all the pilgrims are hanging out in front of the shelter; some sitting on low walls, others reclining on white lawn chairs, others leaning against walls, writing notes, talking, calling their families, or simply resting. Our arrival does not go unnoticed at such a late time of day. We are questioned and have to explain that due to our arrival in Cahors early afternoon, we had to cover the entire distance in the afternoon, when most of them had done it casually throughout the whole day.

We grab a cold beer right from the fridge in the kitchen and sit outside with everyone. Tonight, dinner is served at 7:00 in the dining room, so there is no time to shower before dinner. Oh well, we will survive. Thirteen other pilgrims are staying in this place. The dining room resembles a cave and features a stone, arched low ceiling, where one long table centered and camp-style benches fill the long, narrow room. We dine on a lentil salad to start, a pork stew with prunes, some local cheese and a crumble for dessert. The ambiance is very warm and convivial.

After dinner, the group makes it back outside to enjoy the dark and cool night of a late summer day. Some go for a stroll in the hamlet, while others, in search of phone reception, gather on top of a hill in the middle of the country road—the only good spot, it seems, to make their calls. The sight is sad, yet comical. Indeed, this only and so-limited connection to the rest of the world reminds me of how technology-dependent we have become. This forced retreat from the modern world can become a challenge for some and a relief for others.

Our room is on the second floor at the top of a large, restored, creaky wooden staircase. Tired and a little out of it, we open the door to our bedroom and let out a scream when a furry animal, itself freaked out, scurries out of the room between my legs. A cat! He had snuck in the room through the opened window and was trapped inside.

After this end of the day emotion and a good shower, we gladly climb in bed and snuggle under the warm cover.

*****

The morning dawns wet and damp as we head toward the town of Montcuq. Due to the drizzly rain, we open up our rain poncho and manage to stay dry until we reach Montcuq. Our first stop, at the entrance of the village, is to savor figs right from the tree.

The second stop, just a bit further for a picture in front of the village's entrance sign, features a mandatory smirk on our faces. Why? In French, Montcuq is pronounced the same as *mon cul*, meaning my ass. However, the locals until recently spoke Occitan and the village name, when pronounced correctly, sounds out the 'q' pronounced as 'k,' Mon-cuk. In a well-known joke back in 1976, Daniel Prévost, a French humorist, in the TV show "*Le petit rapporteur*," animated by Jacques Martin, visited the town and joked around by asking the mayor of Montcuq: "Is Montcuq well-lit? Because I've heard that it is sometimes gloomy…" You can find this video on YouTube.

Lying in the beautiful Quercy countryside, Montcuq is a town that has considerable charm with its old stone buildings, a thirteenth century tower and dungeon, and traditional street market. It is a vibrant, agricultural community famed for its gourmet treats such as meringues and waffles.

Meringue, a type of dessert often associated with French cuisine, is made from whipped egg whites and sugar, and encompasses several types of meringues: The sweetened, uncooked beaten egg whites that form the "islands" of Floating Island, known in French as île flo*ttante*; the partly cooked toppings of lemon meringue pie and other meringue-topped desserts, and the classic dry featherweight meringue. Different preparation techniques produce these results; however, French meringue is the method best known to home cooks, where fine white sugar is beaten into egg whites.

We buy a few supplies for lunch and take a break on the terrace of a café, where we enjoy a hot chocolate and a snack while chatting with other pilgrims. The rain has stopped and we can sit outside.

We leave Montcuq by a little road, and after crossing a bridge, we take an uphill trail through the woods and follow the GR 65 signs for another hour before settling for lunch in an opened field overlooking the trail. We are joined by two male bikers, a couple of guys who sit down with us for a while and share a cup of tea.

We resume our journey after an hour, spending the afternoon eating grapes and meeting wild boars on our way to Lauzerte. Lauzerte can be seen from far away, which makes the last miles endless. Indeed, Lauzerte is a fortified medieval town, perched on top of a promontory. Its present name dates back to approximately 1000 AD. Derived from the Latin lucerna, or lamp, it designates an ideal position, visible—like a light—from a distance.

Figure 17: Sunflower Fields

Lauzerte has been listed since April 1990 as one of the Most Beautiful Villages of France, villages selected for the quality of their heritage, their architecture, and their environment. Obtaining this classification involves a rigorous selection process, and retaining it requires constant effort.

Located in the heart of the Chasselas region, a protected designation of origin grape, Lauzerte does indeed look out over a mouth-watering landscape. Its pathways meander between limestone plateaus and gentle valleys. As the seasons unfold, the latter take on the colors of the fruit trees, sunflowers, sweet corn, vines, and lavender.

Our hosts for the night own a nice property at the bottom of the fortified town, on the foothills of the mount. 'Les Figuiers' —The Fig Trees—, the name of the house, is inviting. We are welcomed with a minty drink and homemade biscuits. How thoughtful! It is amusing to notice how receptive we are to the little attentions we kindly receive from strangers.

Once rested and showered, we undertake our visit of the medieval town, which implies more walking and mainly more climbing. We are rewarded by the beautiful center of the village, the place des Cornières, bordered on three sides by three-centered, semi-circular arches and houses dating from the fifteenth to the eighteenth centuries. The upper part of the village is a typical example of medieval city design, with houses arranged around the church of Saint Barthélemy and the main square, Place des Cornières, one of the finest in the region. The ramparts are a reminder of the role played by Lauzerte, alternately seized by the English and the French during the Hundred Years War. Early Gothic or Renaissance houses are a reminder that the medieval city was also much prized by rich magistrates and prosperous merchants. They knew full well how to defend the privilege of their quality of life.

After sipping a beverage under the arches on the terrace of a café, people watching and listening to the Saturday nightlife of the village, we walk down to our home for the night, where diner is awaiting us and six other pilgrims. After an aperitif, a delicious meal is served, composed of: Quercy melon and salad, grilled sausages, green beans and figs, cheese and a homemade pie. Two hours later, we call it a night and retreat to our rooms for a good night's sleep.

*****

We start the day with a breakfast jazzed up with homemade fig jam at 7:00 and hit the road around quarter to eight with the rising sun. This morning, the trail meanders through rich valleys of orchards, where we find peaches, apples, cherries, prunes, along with grapes and kiwis.

We arrive in Durfort mid-morning, where we celebrate our first 400 kilometers (248 miles). Even though it is morning, we stick to the tradition and order a glass of red wine to share, along with two hot chocolates and a *chausson aux pommes*. Unable to finish the wine this early, we pour the rest in a plastic bottle and take it along for lunch. No wine wasting allowed, in a sane French mind.

We arrive in Moissac mid-afternoon, which gives us plenty of time to visit. Moissac is a bigger town compared to what we have been through lately, and we forget how larger towns are surrounded by expansive suburbs. The entry route to the heart of the city takes forever and we start to moan in complaint. Thirty minutes later, we reach the center of town. Today is Sunday, the stores are closed and the streets mostly deserted of pedestrians until we near the heart of the city. This long and unassuming approach is compensated by a beautiful abbatial from the twelfth century. Many hikers have gathered near the abbatial. We find an outdoor café right in front of the church, and are glad to dismount our packs to settle and enjoy our traditional panaché.

Well rested, we set out to look for the place where we will sleep. We have made arrangements to sleep at the Carmel, a religious edifice near the center of town. We leave our bags in our room, remove our heavy hiking boots, put on some flip flops, and return to the center of town to take a tour of the abbatial. The cloister in the abbatial is lovely and so peaceful. More investigation through the city takes us to the *Canal du Midi* and the Tarn River, two waterways drawing tourists and locals alike to their banks.

Dinner is served at 7:15 p.m., so we make our way back to the Carmel to shower, do some laundry and be ready on time. No one wants to upset the nuns. We enjoy the luxury of washing our clothes in a washing machine and even a dryer. It is a luxury we have not been granted for a while! Fourteen of us gather in a dining room adjacent to the cloister. The meal is filling, but it has nothing memorable. The major part of the meal is a frozen dinner with a French twist. We are a little disappointed to realize the nuns are not dining with us, but rather serving us. We were all looking forward to a unique experience, questioning and conversing with them.

At 8:30 p.m., we are asked to leave the room, so we gather in the cloister to discuss tomorrow's optional routes.

*****

We get up early morning to get ready and opt for shorts, since the weather forecast is promising, and grab a quick and frugal breakfast. In discussing our options last night, we decided for the trail that follows the waterway. The other trail climbs to the Boudou and comes right back down. What's the point? We decide that hiking flat, giving some rest to our calves today, will be just fine. We are not on the GR 65, the trail we always follow, but we soon find out there are no risks of taking a wrong turn. The path we are on is embedded between a canal to the right and the Garonne River to the left for a distance of eight miles. Pulling barges along the rivers and canals on towpaths was very common before the invention of engines for boats, which now makes great hiking trails all over Europe.

It is a pretty sight on this early morning. The sun is not out yet when we leave the Carmel, and there is so much moisture in the air that we are surrounded by fog. The scenery, spooky with its tall, thin trees lined up flawlessly and foggy air muffling any distant noise, creates a sensation of being alone, resonate with our sleepy minds. We are witnessing the awakening of nature, quietly by surprise. The spiders who have had all night to weave their delicate webs are resting, content, looking at their artwork. Now that the dew is softly resting on them, it shows each and every delicate turn and twist of the intricate pattern. No one talks except to point out a spider web here or an early morning crane venturing in the shallow water there. We left early and ahead of everyone to embrace this moment of serenity. The trail of Santiago offers many different moments when individuals can simply absorb new sensations, colors and scents, based on the time they roll through it.

The beautifulness of the place eventually fades away as the miles add up. By the time we reach the end of this towpath, which we now perceive as a monotonous trail, the return to a somewhat common itinerary feels good. Our minds were in need of change to find the motivation to move forward. When you walk and all you see is the same landscape straight ahead, with no significant change but a lock here or a boat there, your mind starts to cry out, "Are we there yet?" No regrets, though. It was well worth it, especially early this morning.

We arrive in Pommevic mid-morning, in time for a break. An amicable grandpa indicates a hotel café nearby bordering the highway. We leave the canal and climb up to the road to find the only café in this small village. The service is very poor, and after much patience and insistence, we obtain a hot chocolate, but nothing to eat. As starving as we are from walking for three hours, we opt to get out our own supplies to eat with our hot cocoa, hoping to not offend the waiter. The camembert, this pungent cheese and some leftover baguette will do. A fresh croissant would have been welcome, but a cheese sandwich will quench our hunger.

Back on the trail, we reach the road that will lead us to Auvillar, officially recognized as one of the most beautiful villages of France. The way there is of little interest. We are in the plain of the Garonne River, and the landscape is flat, flat, flat! After following a black-top road for one hour, we consciously start to avoid walking on the black top as much as possible. Our feet are starting to buzz after eight miles of walking this morning. It's a sensation that comes with rhythmical steps on hard surfaces. We look for grass strips that follow the road to soothe our fatigued feet.

Figure 18: The Village of Auvillar

We notice a mount on the horizon. Auvillar is finally in sight. Largely built of local red brick, the village enjoys an imposing view over the Garonne Valley. We enter the village through a gate topped by a red and white brick, square tower called the clock tower from the seventeenth century. The Place de la Halle is an unusual triangular "square" with a stunning circular grain market at its heart. The *Halle aux Graines* is a must see with its Tuscan columns and Roman tiled roof, and its fascinating stone medieval and metal nineteenth-century grain measures.

The quaint village offers a few restaurants to choose from. We select one located under plane trees, near the clock tower. The building, keeping the harmonious architectural style of the village, is made out of white stone and red brick, and opens up onto a shady terrace, away from the traffic and tourists. The season for porcini is at its peak, and the menu proposes again a porcini omelet served with a salad topped with goat cheese. A glass of cool rosé wine with that and we drag this halt for an hour and a half.

Let me tell you that after this divine stop, we are stiff, unmotivated and lazy … rosé wine can do that! The good news is that we only have five miles to cover this afternoon; about two hours and we should be there.

Our arrival in Saint Antoine is eased by the fact that it is a minuscule hamlet, anciently founded by the Antonins religious order that ran a hospital on the road to St. James. Today, the hamlet consists of one street and a few houses, a pilgrim's dormitory, a bar-restaurant, and a small, but colorful church with a flat church tower. When we arrive, all the pilgrims are already settled in, wearing their evening outfits, for the most part, a pair of shorts, t-shirt and comfortable flip flops. They are busy getting their gear ready for tomorrow, hanging laundry outside to dry in the large courtyard or lingering on the lawn chairs in the late afternoon sun. The gite is a rehabilitated farm, composed of three buildings, a large court in front, and a stone surrounding wall.

Our bedroom, reserved earlier, is private but that is the only positive aspect; we are adjacent to the large shed where the tractors are kept. There are no windows and only enough room to fit two single, blue metal hospital-like types of beds, two chairs and a night stand. We decide to nickname it "the closet." We slip in our evening outfit after a quick shower, and leave to investigate the hamlet before dark. The little street is paved and runs through the middle of the houses, which are decorated with hanging flower baskets from the balconies. The café is open with a couple of tables outside, right in the middle of the road. It is definitely a pedestrian road, so we can't resist the temptation to sit back and order a refreshing panaché.

Our visit finished, we head back to the gite at the end of the road. The whole crew is gathered outside around a large oval table, chatting or writing, with filled tea pots and hazelnuts, freshly handpicked during the day by a pilgrim. Tonight the crew is dining out in the restaurant in town at 7:00. A long table, covered with red paper tablecloths set in a rustic large room, has been prepared to accommodate all of us; a group of fifteen pilgrims, mainly French, coming from all regions.

*****

Today, Tuesday, we are the first ones to leave around 7:30 a.m. and head toward Lectoure, our evening stop only fourteen miles away. Along the way, castles here and there are being renovated, depicting a style from the fifteenth century, when the harshness of the fortified castles was fading away.

Through farm fields, hills and valleys, what we encounter is what makes this adventure so unique and special. A generous and thoughtful farmer, gone to work for the day, has left a table, set with a colorful printed tablecloth, on the edge of his field, a couple of steps away from the path, under a tree providing shade, and a wooden, homemade bench offering a perfect resting spot. The table is garnished with water, red wine, bread, hard boiled eggs and tomatoes. All the basic needs a pilgrim might need: shade from the hot sun, a bench to rest, water to quench his thirst, food for energy and wine to warm up his heart. We are not ready to make an official stop, but decide to take a couple of hard boiled eggs for our later lunch in exchange for a couple of coins left in a jar at the center of the table, as a token of our appreciation.

Figure 19: A Table Set for the Pilgrims on the Side of the Trail

We are almost in Miradoux, known for its Middle Age history. We make a stop at the bakery and pharmacy, and continue our route. A dog, eager to go for a walk, accompanies us as we exit the village. We are worried that he will get lost or run over, since we are following a busy country road where people tend to drive a little too fast. All our efforts are pointless. He does not listen to us and only walks ahead of us and seems to be waiting for us, looking back and slowing down, as if he was showing us the way. We quickly understand that he probably does this regularly and indeed does know the way, as he makes each turn as if reading the GR 65 signs. His master finally catches up to us in a utility car, and almost as a routine, tells him to hop in to go home. Waving and smiling, he lowers his window and confirms that his dog loves to go walking with the pilgrims as they come by.

We arrive later on in Castet-Arouy, a village where we had planned to buy supplies for lunch. According to the icons in the book, a little shopping cart indicating food supplies, there should be a store somewhere. To our distress, there is nothing around. We are starving and it is almost lunch time. What are we going to do? We do have a couple of hard boiled eggs from the farmer's table earlier, but surely this is not enough to keep us going all day! A few pilgrims are eating their lunch, a lunch they carried all day or even bought at the prior town, sitting in the middle of the square in front of the Gothic-style church. We think for a minute to go beg for a thing or two, but hesitantly we hold off, still hoping for a solution.

That's when we catch a glimpse of a man entering a closed hotel-restaurant, and hasten toward him to plead for food. We explain our situation and ask him if he has a few basic items we can buy from him. This good-natured and sensible man takes pity on us and kindly gives us a whole salami, four large slices of ham and two tomatoes. Sympathetic, he only accepts two Euros from us and sends us on our way, wishing us a *Bon Chemin*.

Figure 20: La Romieu Cloister

Shortly after leaving Castet-Arouy, we start looking for a lunch place to sit down. The sun is out, and we can't wait to eat what we have gathered through our morning's encounters.

Five miles to go before Lectoure, which should bring us there early enough to do some sightseeing. La Romieu, a walled town, founded by two monks back from a pilgrimage to Rome in 1062, is a must see in the area. The magnificent collegiate church and cloister have been listed since 1998 as a world heritage by UNESCO. A taxi ride away and we are there.

As one walks through the village, you can't fail to notice the sculptures of cats on window ledges and wonder what the story is behind this. A legend: Angeline and the Legend of the Cats.

In the year 1338, Vincent and Mariette lived contentedly. Vincent was a woodman and his wife often accompanied him into the forest to make up bundles. They worked hard, and with their poultry and pig, and fruit and vegetable garden, their table was always laid full with food.

They had been married for three years when Mariette gave birth to a little girl they named Angeline. Alas, one day Vincent was crushed by a falling tree. Inconsolable, Mariette sank into a depression and two months later was found dead, holding little Angeline in her arms. The little girl was brought up by a neighbor.

Angeline showed a great affection for cats and there were always one or two around her, which at night even slept in her bed. She also often shared her bowl of food with them. In 1342 and the two years that followed, the winters were harsh and the springs and summers so wet that it was impossible to sow crops. Then followed a great famine, and in spite of the distribution of the collegiate reserves by the lord Arnaud d'Aux, the inhabitants soon had nothing left to eat. They thought of the numerous cats in the village and set about catching them.

Angeline's adoptive parents, knowing how much she loved hers, allowed her to keep a male and female cat on the condition she hid them well, as the neighbors would gladly kill them. Angeline, therefore, enclosed her two cats in the attic during the day and at night she let them out to hunt. But the famine grew worse and many villagers died. Angeline and her parents barely subsisted by collecting roots in the woods and sometimes they found mushrooms, but it was hardly sufficient. Weakened by hunger, they managed somehow to survive this terrible period and more clement times finally arrived, allowing them to harvest what they needed to live on.

But in La Romieu, where the cats had disappeared, rats proliferated to a point where the crops were once again threatened. Angeline, with infinite caution, had been able to hide her cats in the attic and they had produced several young kittens. There were now about twenty of these cats. The villagers wrung their hands over the damage caused by the rats. Angeline announced that she was going to release some twenty cats, which the inhabitants would be able to adopt. The rats rapidly disappeared and it is thus that Angeline resembled more and more, with the passing of time, one of her cats, her ears looking more and more like the ears of a cat.

Back in Lectoure, we are eager to spend some time in our room, a lavish place, decorated in elegant style, situated on the main strip. We climb two flights of circular, wooden stairs leading to a long, wooden floor hallway and the entrance of the apartment. Warm tones of orange, red, pink and sage immensely contrast with last night's white walls of the so-called "closet." The blankets are fluffy and the towels provided, an obvious call to take advantage of the situation and indulge in a bath.

Lectoure, located in the Gers, is known for its Armagnac, a brandy, foie gras and duck or goose delicacies. Also the *Floc de Gascogne*, another specialty of this area, is an Armagnac-based aperitif.

Informed ahead on the trails that Lectoure was indeed the place to stop to satisfy the gourmet palate, we are determined to find a good table for diner and definitely avoid the traditional pilgrim menu. We find a table at L'Auberge des Bouviers, a traditional restaurant down the street from our lodging. Starting with a glass of Floc de Gascogne, followed by pan-fried foie gras for appetizer, and duck confit for main course, we are delighted with this gastronomic experience.

*****

Up and ready at 7:00, we head downstairs to the street and buy a few supplies before breakfast, served at 7:30. Our stage today will take us to

Condom, a little over nineteen miles. The weather is rainy and the wind is brutally cold, which keeps us walking non-stop for five miles; a little over two hours to the little town of Marsolan, which has no warm place for us to sit. So we take a break on the square in front of the church and gather with other pilgrims we met earlier. A quick snack and we are on our way, as trying to stay warm is the priority today.

We decide to avoid la Romieu, which we visited last night, and most of us choose to take the shortcut. Except for one man, to whom we say goodbye as we know he will not catch up. The trail is not marked and it makes these next few kilometers a little tricky to navigate.

By now, we have met a few people and it is fun to run into them here and there. Two girls from Lille, met back in Moissac, join us for lunch in a sunny field. I have the bright idea to lay a survival blanket to sit on to serve as a clean cover and keep my pants mud-free. The silvery shiny sheet attracts heat, as it is meant to do, which feels wonderful. In a short time, my mother looks at me puzzled.

"You look like a crawfish," she giggles. Glancing at the shiny sheet, I realize my poor decision. Sitting on a survival blanket is not a good idea unless you are looking for a quick tan.

In Condom, we stay at an American friend's house who is not here at the moment, but has arranged that a friend visiting from Australia welcomes us. The village house, with periwinkle blue shutters, is centrally located and directly across from La Baïse River. Built on two stories, the house is roomy and even has a private, walled-in backyard. It is charming.

Tonight, after browsing in town, we find another good restaurant, and since we are celebrating our first 500 kilometers (310 miles), we again indulge and eat foie gras and lamb shank. This year is turning into a gourmet tour—to my delight.

Figure 21: 1,003 kilometers to go

*****

Today is another big day, with twenty-one miles to reach our evening destination, Eauze. We quietly leave the house at 7:00, with our backpacks and bourdons, and stop in at the restaurant next door for breakfast. Another stop at the bakery down the street, and by 7:30, we head out to exit the town. We bump into two male acquaintances, Pierre and Jean-Lou, from the trail and start hiking together. The pace with them is fast, but it is not a bad thing today considering the mileage we have to cover. It will keep us on track. The weather is still cold, but it is better than the forecast.

We are traveling through the vineyards, and it is the grape-harvesting season. We are in luck today and can witness the picking of Madame Eliane's vineyard, a white grape called Colombar. The machines have a funny shape. High on wheels, they have a square body that allows them to fit through the well-kept rows of vines, collecting the grapes without damaging the vineyards. We watch the whole process until the tub of the machine empties its load of freshly picked, plump white Colombar grapes in a truck that will take them to their winemaking facility.

Energized from this new experience, we restart our pilgrimage toward new discoveries. Every day brings new life lessons, especially for two city girls. Our foursome is getting hungry; it is damp, the sky is overcast, and we are cold. It only takes us a mere kilometer to run into an interesting spectacle. On the left inside of the road, we discern an older couple in the distance, sitting comfortably on a couple of chairs, right next to a tall concrete milepost. They appear to be dressed for the weather and reading the newspaper. Intriguing! As we get closer, we discover the catch: the adorable old couple, wearing a shawl and a fancy hat, is indeed fabricated and welcomes passengers who might be looking for a warm plate of food or a bed for the night. We see our fate in this unexpected finding and Joelle invites us into her home.

Once rid of our dirty attire, we make our way into her living room and settle into comfortable, cushiony couches adjacent to an old-fashioned, lit-up fireplace. There, in the hearth of the fireplace, is a large, light blue kettle keeping the soup warm. In no time, the dishes are brought and the country-style hearty soup, la *Garbure Gasconne*, is served. What a joy! This typical country soup from the southwest is filled with cabbage, ham, goose, sausages, turnips and potatoes, carrots, onions, and clove, varying according to the seasonal vegetables. Conversations, unexpected warmth and food make this moment memorable.

La Garbure

Serves: 4-6

Ingredients

- ½ lb of salt pork belly, chop into large chunks
- 6 oz of smoked raw ham
- 6 pieces of duck confit
- 1 bouquet garni
- ½ lb of white beans (soaked overnight if dried)
- 2 leeks (trimmed, slit and washed, the white plus about 2 inches of green)
- ½ lb of potatoes, (peeled and roughly chopped)
- 4 sticks of celery (trimmed, washed and chopped)
- 3 small white turnips (peeled, washed and chopped)
- 1 large onion, roughly chopped
- 4 garlic cloves (peeled)
- 1 small cabbage (shredded)

- salt and pepper
- 3 pints of water
- 1 small onion stuck with 2 cloves

Method:
Add pork belly and beans to the water, bring to the boil, skimming frequently add the onion with cloves and turn down to a simmer for about 1 hour
meanwhile take the leeks, onion and sweat down till softened, add to the soup along with the tunips, the bouquet garni and some salt and pepper simmer for another 45 mins discard the onion with cloves
add the potatoes and the smoked ham, bring back to a boil then reduce to a simmer for 30 mins
finally add the confit and the cabbage, and simmer for another 20-30 mins
eat with thick slices of French country bread

Joelle quickly brings to our attention that all the pilgrimage stops in Eauze are full. Our reservation in a hotel, made this morning, was a great idea. We can keep walking without worrying about where we will sleep tonight. Our two companions who have not booked anything for tonight are a bit concerned, but grateful for the notice.

Saying our goodbyes to Joelle, we set out to walk toward new adventures. With the comfortable couches in mind, this makes for a definite hard restart. We make a quick stop to purchase tomatoes and shredded seasoned carrots for lunch. Around 12:30 p.m., we find a field and the four of us luncheon for forty-five minutes.

Figure 22: Friendly Donkeys

It is with great surprise that in the afternoon, we reconnect with three pilgrims, lost earlier this morning when the trail was poorly marked. They are hungry and tired, but glad to see known faces.

The rest of the afternoon is uneventful. Observant of our surroundings and making mental notes of the regional specificities, we notice how the traditional houses are adapted to the weather, facing and open to the southern or eastern sun, while mainly closed to the west and north, protecting themselves from the cold and wind. The last stretch before Eauze, about four miles, takes place on an old train track path, bordered with thick trees on each side, where it is possible to stop for a cup of hot tea and cookies, which we do.

We finally arrive in Eauze late afternoon and locate our hotel quickly, thanks to the help of the tourism office. Our hotel, Triana, offers a meal that is not suiting what we have in mind tonight. We have been spoiled the last couple of nights with local specialties, and we intend to continue our gourmet tour of Le Gers. After a glass of Floc, our new evening drink, at a neighborhood café, we find a restaurant in the center of town and savor an *assiette gourmande*, a large platter composed of duck foie gras, smoked duck breast thinly sliced, warm confit duck gizzards, served on a bed a crispy greens with toasted country bread.

*****

Friday, our last day for this year, is beautiful. The sun is out and the sky is blue everywhere, with no clouds in sight. Our morning in the hotel starts a bit tense. As hotel guests, we have an appointed table set for two for breakfast, and it is our fault for not noticing it behind an animated table, so we sit down at a table set for five. Our waitress is very upset with us as we have disturbed her morning routine. We apologize and prepare for our day. With only twelve miles to Nogaro, we take our time and depart around 8:00.

En route, we walk by a duck farm, where hundreds of ducklings are walking around in the grass. What a sight! The rising sun is just peaking from behind the tree line and shines onto the farm. I can't resist leaning over the ditch to get closer to the electrical fence in order to take a close-up shot without the metal fencing in the way. The morning dew is covering the fence, and even though I am wearing gloves, when I touch the fence with my pinkie, I am literally thrown backward. These ducklings are definitely well-protected.

Later on, after a stop to fix a bleeding toe of mine, we are walking on a little road, with some trees on our right and a large pond, l'Etang de Pouy, to our left, when suddenly, we are under attack. Stopped in the middle of the road, we bend down to see what our aggressor looks like. Raised on his back legs, arms wide open, our red little fellow is on the defense. His pinchers, all opened and ready to attack, are pointed at us. Crossing the road going back to the pond, he has felt the vibration on the road from our hiking sticks. We learned later in our guide book that this is a fish farming area, most specifically a crawfish farm. We laugh at the brave little soldier and resume our walk.

In Manciet, after a hot chocolate at the café, we catch up to our new friends, met a couple of days ago. We take farewell pictures, exchange email addresses and phone numbers as they will be going on with their adventure, but we will stop in Nogaro in six miles.

Our last stretch is cut short, as we decide to stay on the road and avoid a detour. We have been slowly moving this morning, and we have to meet a taxi in Nogaro to drive back to Agen, where we will catch our train for Paris.

The road is quicker, straighter, but rolling all the way to Nogaro. We realize we are near when we start hearing engines roaring ahead. Nogaro is home to a famous race track. The Circuit Paul Armagnac is a motorsport race track, built in 1960. The venue hosted the French round of the Grand Prix motorcycle road racing world championship in 1978 and 1982, as well as more recently the FIA GT Championship held in 2012.

We arrive in the center of town just in time to sit down and have lunch before our taxi appointment at 2 o'clock in front of the church. The trip is resting and takes about an hour and a half. For a while, we can follow our steps backward, as Agen is situated to the north of Lectoure. An hour and a half to cover three hiking days. Back to reality and the modern world.

In Agen, we entrust our backpacks to the kind station master, and we are free to browse around in town. Our train is not scheduled to arrive before 6:38 p.m., so we take the time to visit a bit. We also buy some porcini, enough to make a whole platter, from a local farmer selling his harvest on the sidewalk.

The speed train, TGV, takes us back to Paris Montparnasse after one week on the *Chemin*. One more year behind us, more acquaintances and the beginning of *Radio Chemin*, a radio run by people, by word of mouth, by noticeable traits, attitudes, or origins. We are quickly identified as the mother-daughter girls, the panaché lovers, and also the same t-shirt group. Indeed, we had started back in the beginning to wear the same color shirt every day, picked from this wide fashionable selection carried in our backpack; black, red or orange. It was a year notable for the gustatory indulgences proper to the Gers region.

Year Four

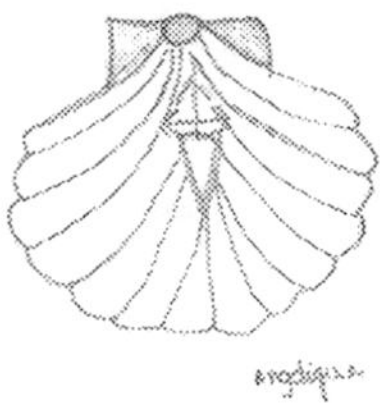

From Nogaro to Roncevaux
126 miles in 8 days

"I can do all things through him who strengthens me."
Philippians 4:13

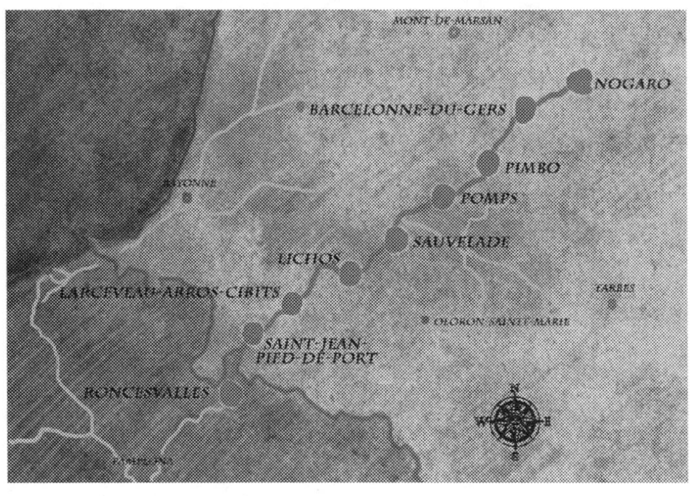

Freshly arrived from the American Midwest, midday on Thursday, we enjoy going over our gear, comparing and deciding on last-minute necessities.

We get up bright and early Friday to catch a 6:10 a.m. train at Gare Montparnasse, on the left bank in Paris, a forty-minute drive from our house in the west suburbs. Even though it is so early, the train is packed. We eat breakfast served right in our seat, airplane mode. We're too lazy to go to the bar, instead wanting to doze off a bit in prevision of the sixteen miles of hiking we will have to accomplish upon arrival.

Our train had to make a stop in the middle of the countryside for over twenty-five minutes due to a medical issue on board. When we arrive in Nogaro, our taxi driver, reserved from Paris, is expecting us and is well aware of the delay.

Eager to catch up, the taxi driver is a little zealous and drives quite fast on these small, sinuous country roads. But as promised, we arrive in Nogaro right where we left off last year, in front of Saint Nicolas Collegiate Church, at the same time we had arrived last year, 12:30 p.m.

We are still in the Gers, surrounded by corn and sunflower fields, with not much visibility. The day goes by fast. As always with the excitement of the first day, we seem to fly. Not a village in sight, but a homemade rest area welcomes us. *Bienvenue, Gardez le Moral*, halfway through, features a wooden bench and picnic tables set along the side of the path, decorated with scallops' sea shells, the symbol of the trail. We are back on the trail and it feels good.

It feels so good that we pass our planned stopping point and add on a few miles to arrive in a village called Barcelone sur Gers around 7 p.m. We find a hotel, Chez Alain, where dinner is served at 8 p.m. Our bedroom, across the street in a two-story, narrow building, is clean but basic; a sink and a shower. Unfortunately, the one toilet is located on the first floor. Who is going to go down in the middle of the night for a bathroom break? Not me; I would rather hold it.

Cleaned up, we head down and cross the street. The place looks closed up, but we knock and wait hopefully. Someone opens the door and we enter into a dining room filled with a handful of guests already eating. We are late and have missed the local aperitif: a drink called d'Artagnan, a mixture of Armagnac, orange and a Sprite-like soda. Upon our arrival, we are asked to sit down and food arrives instantly from the kitchen. A delicious whole tureen of chunky vegetable soup is served, followed by an omelet with herbs leading to the main course. Ham, leg of lamb, and vegetables are next. To end this gargantuan meal, ice cream is served. What a feast for this first day! Except that we have not built-up such a large appetite yet—we are still on regular city mode.

It is easy to imagine that it does not take much for us to fall asleep. We find just enough energy to climb the two floors to our room and write in our diary to record some of the details encountered today.

*****

We rise, have breakfast and leave by 8:30 a.m. We are only a couple of miles away from Aire sur l'Adour, a mid-size town. We enter the town by crossing l'Adour, a wide river, on a wide bridge decorated with flags over the water, and pink geraniums hanging all along.

It is Saturday morning, and the town is lively and pleasant. A nice change from yesterday's deserted paths. A pedestrian street crosses the town and leads to the indoor market, swarming with people. We can't help ourselves from going inside to see the local produce. We overbuy a bit, but cannot resist the call of the market. We find cheese, country *saucisson*, a rustic type of summer sausage with apparent chunks of meat and fat, and a sweet-smelling cantaloupe. Once loaded, we decide that the heavy melon will have to be eaten sooner than later.

As we leave Aire, we lose track of the trail markings and can't seem to find our way until a helpful older man comes to our rescue. He explains that due to a regional plan of reconstruction, the Chemin has been a bit disturbed and that he has been watching, because pilgrims can't find their way.

The worse part of the story is that we are now walking, literally, on the side of a fast road, where cars and trucks are passing by us at full speed. There really is not a path for us, only the pathway made by the many other hikers forced to use this way. More than three miles, a good hour, at a good pace, one behind each other, watching incoming traffic, is not a bit enjoyable. Walking into the incoming traffic, we use our stick to keep cars from cutting us short, or we jump into the ditch when semis drive by as we can feel a draft pulling us onto the road.

Mid-morning, it is warm enough that we can remove our fleece and our leggings. Shorts and t-shirts it is. What a change from last year. Our stop for lunch is among the vines, in the middle of a white grape vineyard. It is hot and we have some shade from the vine as we sit on the grass. We can finally feast on the cantaloupe with saucisson and cheese.

Miramont, the planned stop for the night, is not a good option. It is too early to stop, so we continue to the next village, Pimbo, a couple of hours away. Pimbo is a tiny little village, located on a promontory around its abbey. Upon arrival, we locate the gite right away, only to find out all five beds already are accounted for. There is, of course, an extra mattress which can be set on the floor and a couch in the entrance that we are encouraged to use. But we are not quite up for this after twenty miles, and on top of it all, we have not planned for food. We decide to investigate the village and see if we can find a room to rent.

Unfortunately, the whole village is celebrating a marriage. Irène's son, a young fellow, is willing to help. Dressed for the wedding, he offers to drive us to the next village where there is a hotel. We are saved. Arsacq Arraziguet is not as quaint as Pimbo, but we are in luck and the hotel, la Vieille Auberge, has one room left. Close call!

The room is as small as last night, with a sink and a mini-shower, but all in all it is acceptable and even has a toilet hidden behind a partition.

Tomorrow is Sunday and all retailers will be closed, except for the bakery in the morning. We need to get a few items for the road at the grocery store and the pharmacy. Planning for necessities is so different than what we have to deal with back home. Here, we worry about finding a roof at night, filling our stomach three times a day, and staying healthy, before surrendering to the moment.

*****

This morning, we need to figure out where we will sleep tonight. Last night had its share of adventure, but today let's try to be a little more prepared. Originally, we had seen in our book that there were beds with new beddings and showers in a gymnasium. We discuss the matter at breakfast with a pilgrim who brings to our attention the existence of a bed and breakfast in Pomps. We hasten to contact Bernard and Sylvie, the owners, who sadly inform us they have no room available, but suggest getting in contact with the last people who book their last room, which can accommodate two more people. It is worth the try! Comically, the other pilgrims are the two men we were talking to at breakfast. They are totally okay with the idea of sharing.

Remaining true to hiking the accurate mileage, we take a taxi back to Pimbo. Cheating is not an option! Pimbo is quiet on this Sunday morning;

the whole village is sleeping, recovering from the late night at the wedding. The sun is rising slowly, lighting up the fields. We can hear the rooster calling, but this morning the village will sleep in.

We have a difficult passage on the way to Arsacq. My mom is deadly afraid of chickens or any feathery animals, for that matter. The hens this morning are not in the hen house; at least thirty of them are loose walking around on the road, scattered on each side, picking worms and any insects they can find. Despite their beautiful, rich colors–brown, black, white and orangey tone feathers—my mother does not see the prettiness in them. Hiding behind me as close as possible, she makes it through, avoiding running chickens and we arrive safely in Arsacq, with no chicken pecks.

We picnic in the middle of nature again, in a field, in the sun, away from the path. Taking our time, as usual, the scenery is inviting for a mini-nap. But it is time to pick up and go.

In Uzan, a sign catches our attention with a scallop sea shell, inviting pilgrims to enter the yard for a rest, coffee and more:

"Pèlerins en chemin pour Compostelle, vous trouverez café...thé...eau... entrez...et...servez-vous. Bonne route..."

Figure 23: Supporting the Pilgrims - Private Home

In the back yard, a picnic table and chairs, shadowed by a green and yellow umbrella, welcome pilgrims. In the corner, beverages and desserts are for all to enjoy. This is a real pleasure to see how supportive some of these villagers are.

We are still making our way to our next stop in the afternoon when the phone beeps. Our host, Bernard, has been trying to call us ten times, but due to bad reception, we had not heard a thing. He has been worrying and wondering where we were. He insists on coming to get us even though we are almost there, as he wants to take us on a tour.

Their property is very nice; the main house, made out of white stones has blue periwinkle shutters. Our room is in a side building, all renovated and stylish. The large room we share with the two men is separated in the middle by one bathroom.

Before dinner, our host takes us on a guided tour to visit the nearby village and fourteenth century castle of Morlanne, a heptagonal brick fortress.

*****

We get up early and get ready quietly. Our neighbors have a short stage today and decided to sleep in. After breakfast, Bernard drives us back to where the trail is. By now it is a little after 8 a.m., the sun is peaking far away in the countryside. The road is deserted, sunken between raised fields of corn. The lush, flourishing vegetation is covered with morning dew.

Near a Roman-style chapel, La Chapelle de Caubin, we pause and eat fresh figs that we handpicked right from the tree this morning. So tasty!

We take our break mid-morning in the company of two hikers from Québec in a pilgrim's way stop. The nearby community has kindly organized a quaint area especially for the needs of pilgrims. Tall and awkward benches have been designed to accommodate backpacks so pilgrims don't have to bend down to take off, and mostly, put back on their backpacks; a clever and very convenient concept. Sticks and backpacks taken care of, we sit down at a table and share stories with the two Canadians. Their accent is so strong and unique, it is fun to converse with them.

We pass Arthès de Béarn, then Argagnon to arrive in Maslacq, after crossing the Gave de Pau, a term used for rivers in the southwest of France.

The Gave de Pau is known for passing through Lourdes, carrying the miraculous waters from their source in Lourdes. Throughout the day, we start to notice a change in the landscape. There are more hills, and in the distance, we catch a glimpse for the first time of the chain of the Pyrénées Mountains, the natural border with Spain.

Figure 24: The Pyreness Mountains in the distance

An interesting encounter with a farmer leads to a conversation about his industrial production of green beans for a famous brand in France, Bonduel. We learn that it only takes twenty-four hours from harvest to canned goods. Surprising for a little producer isolated in the hills.

Another encounter, more furry and cuddly, confirms that we are approaching the Pyrénées. At the top of a hill, in the middle of nowhere, a farmhouse is planted there, overlooking the meadows and fields, and a thigh-high, tall white long-haired dog welcomes us. During your walks in the mountains, you are likely to encounter large, white dogs of impressive bulk. Often called "pastous" or "patous," they mix with the flock of sheep and assure its protection.

This breed, called le Chien de Montagne des Pyrénées in French and Great Pyrenees in English, is considered a part of the mountain patrimony. Used in France until the end of the nineteenth century, it has gradually disappeared from these mountains as the large predators—bears, wolves and lynx—have become rare. The natural return of wolves in the Mercantour and the reintroduction of bears in the central Pyrenees have stimulated a renewal of interest in this type of guard dog.

The term "pastou," pronounced patou, is derived from the word "pastre," meaning shepherd in old French and designates a shepherd's dog as it was understood in times past. Unlike a herd dog, the role of the guard dog is not to drive the sheep, but rather to protect them from wild animals or feral dogs. Usually walking at the head of the flock, the patou inspects the terrain before the arrival of the sheep, then establishes a zone of protection around the flock that allows him to anticipate the approach of any intruder.

The famous French movie "Belle et Sébastien," based on the novel by Cécile Aubry, features a patou in a moving story between Belle, a Pyrenean mountain dog, and Sébastien, a six-year-old boy, during World War II.

After a luncheon in a cornfield, lying in the sun, shoes off, shorts on, we head out to our evening shelter. Sauvelade, a large, two-story graying stone masonry, is an abbey founded in 1128. It is where we will sleep and dine. There is literally nothing else in the village. The hamlet IS the old abbey.

Today, September 29, is Saint Michel, so we celebrate my mother's saint day, her *fête*. Once cleaned up, we locate a table with two chairs, outside in the corner of two sheltering walls, in the warm sun. We order an aperitif, a local beer with red tones, to start and quench our thirst, and pursue with a glass of Jurançon wine, and linger until dinner.

The Jurançon, a white wine with a nutty flavor, is an amber-colored wine which can be dry or mellow, and is well-known for it was used to baptize King Henri IV.

The roomy *hostal* incorporates a dining room and a bar, among the usual amenities. Our Swedish-style room is small, but clean and bright thanks to a large window that opens onto the courtyard.

At dinner, gathered around the dining room table, the atmosphere among the guests is convivial. A large group of pilgrims, men and women from Germany, Switzerland, and France, a total of thirteen, are sharing supper, made by a talkative mother while her children, sitting at a table adjacent to ours near the kitchen, do their homework.

*****

The day is late to start since the sun barely rises around 7:45 a.m., so we depart with the sunrise. We have heard many times how some people, mostly in Spain, eager to arrive early at the gite to ensure a bed for the night, will leave early morning, in the dark, using a head lamp to light the path and signage showing the way. In summer, this strategy is also linked to the feared hot sun in some parts of Spain. For us, traveling in fall has eased these restricting aspects, and so we have decided to leave at daybreak to enjoy the scenery.

This morning, the three-hour walk to Navarrenx is uneventful; the roads and trails are simple, and we find a mere bench in a park to sit for our mid-morning pause. We crossed Navarrenx in its length, through the *centre-ville*, where locals are hurrying from one store to the other to buy their groceries for lunch. We grab a couple of items for later and notice that people in the stores are not very friendly, almost irritated with us pilgrims, who are cumbersome and spend little as we can only carry little.

The city, a fortified bastion from the Middle Ages, still displays some vestiges of the ramparts and city doors, in particular a known one used by the pilgrims called The Door of Spain.

We pursue our day following trails in the woods where some men are working, cutting woods and completing other chores. The woods endlessly go on and on until lunch time; we need to locate a spot for a break. We find a bare field, covered with little stems sticking up from the ground –a freshly cut corn field. Our *pareo* becomes handy to provide a clean and soft space to sit and organize our picnic. Isolated, with no cell phone reception, one funny look, one odd noise, and it is not long until we share our feminine intuition. We gobble up our lunch and bail out, commenting on how isolated and remote this place is, reminiscing all these men working on who knows what in the woods. Paranoia! Maybe, but when two women start sharing these feelings, it is catchy.

By midafternoon, we reach the top of a hill where a road leads to a wooden porch roof, covering two large picnic tables with attached benches. A descriptive board adorns the place, and a shelf is loaded with cans of local pâtés that one can buy and taste. This is unexpected and quite pleasant. Snacking right here in front of this mountain range we expect to ascend in a few days is the perfect place to let our minds wander and prepare for the upcoming challenge.

Later on, surrounded by woods, we notice a house perched in the trees, way up high. A little further, men are talking and gathering at the bottom of another tree. Carrying their threatening weapons, I dare interrupt their lively conversation to find out what they might be hunting.

"Good day! We noticed these odd-looking tree houses perched up in the trees. What are they used for?"

"This region is big on hunting ringdoves," he replies.

"What is that?" I ask.

"A wood pigeon, tasty to eat," he smirks. "We sit in the trees nestled in the 'palombières' from where we hunt."

"Make sure to keep your voices down as you walk away," another one adds.

Our arrival in Lichos, a village of 130 inhabitants, is a bit delayed due to a lack of indications when the trail was diverted to avoid going through a farm court. Every once in a while, recent local changes have taken place, but have not made it into the latest editions of the hiking guides. So improvisation becomes a natural skill.

Tonight we are sleeping at Mr. and Mrs. Croharé's house, him a corn farmer and her a retired social studies teacher. They are very welcoming, as well as their home. Our room, decorated in ancient style and adorned with a fireplace, is so comfortable and large with its private bathroom, including all items found at home. A hair dryer is there to use, so we indulge in a beauty session. Taking our time, we then go explore the village and the church; yes, a church even for one hundred thirty inhabitants. The homemade copious dinner, served in the family dining room, makes for a mirthful evening with the family.

*****

Our host gives us good advice on what route to take today, even though it is not following the traditional GR 65. It is a shortcut, saving one mile and reducing the stage to eighteen miles. As soon as the sun is out, around

7:45 a.m., we say our goodbyes to our charming hosts and tackle this new day. The weather is uncertain; it is grey and shortly into our morning, a few drops force us to take out our long-sleeve, army green ponchos.

As we leave the Béarn to enter the Basque Country, we are welcomed with a hand-written poster, in French and in Basque, promoting the beauty of the region.

The Basques primarily inhabit an area traditionally known as the Basque Country, a region that is located around the western end of the Pyrenees on the coast of the Bay of Biscay, straddling parts of northcentral Spain and southwestern France. The Pyrenees Mountains are the major geographic feature of the Basque Country. The traditional Basque house, called Extea, is one of the most unique aspects of a visit to this area. The architectural style, dating back to the seventeenth and eighteenth centuries, consists of starched white façades marked by dark accents of brown, green, burgundy or navy timbers. Basque farms can be seen scattered like so many red and white dots throughout the verdant countryside. Houses are often grouped around the fronton (a large wall used for ball sports) and the church, forming attractive villages. Basque houses blend into the countryside and their names often reflect the local topography. Each house is identified by a name handed down from generation to generation, and quite often, the people living in a house are known by its name.

Figure 25: A Typical Basque Farm

The cuisine remains rural, and in many households, they eat the produce they breed, grow or process at home. Pork produce holds pride of place, and the Espelette pepper is the favorite spice. This traditional cuisine can be enjoyed in restaurants in the form of traditional dishes such as the piperade, the axoa, and the Basque cake. During the wood pigeon hunting season, restaurants serve the flambéed wood pigeon coated with melted fat poured from the capuchin, a conical ladle specific to the region. From October to mid-November, one should reserve a table ahead in order to enjoy this highly prized delicacy.

Basque Cake

Serves: 6

Ingredients:

Dough:

- 1 egg
- 1 egg yolk
- 2 cups flour
- 10 Tb. salted butter
- 1 cup sugar
- 1 lemon
- 1/2 tsp. salt

Cream:

- 1 cup milk
- 2 egg yolks
- 1 egg
- 1/4 cup flour
- 1 Tb. unsalted butter
- 1/4 cup sugar
- 1/2 vanilla bean
- 1 tsp. Rum

Method:

Grate the zest from the lemon. Mix the lemon zest, the egg, the egg yolk, the sugar and the salt in a bowl for the dough.

Beat the mixture, adding slowly the butter, and then the flour. Knead the dough with your hands and roll it into a ball. Let it rest in a fridge for one hour.
Combine the milk and the vanilla bean in a pan and bring to a boil. Remove the bean.

Beat the sugar and egg yolks. Stir in the flour and the rum. Add slowly the hot milk. Cook the mixture over very low heat stirring regularly. Remove from the heat when it begins to boil and add the butter. Let the cream cool.

Preheat the oven at 380 F.

Butter a round oven pan. Roll out two third of the pastry and line the bottom and sides of the pan. Fill with the cream. Cover with the remaining pastry.

Beat an egg and using a brush, coat the top of the cake. Bake in the oven for 45 minutes.

Little by little, we step away from the cornfields, to enter a region of animal breeding, with luxuriant, green, hilly valleys, and baby sheep and veal with their mothers in the fields.

Today is a special day, for we have a rendezvous with someone from Paris. My uncle, Alain, who had a cardiac incident a couple of days before our initial departure four years ago, and his wife, Danièle, are meeting with us to spend two days together. They will be hiking parts of the trails and scouting ahead by car to decide on meeting points.

We are glad to see them walking toward us near Uhart Mixe, where they have found a place for a picnic. Talk about a picnic! Thank God no one had to carry it, because the picnic turned into a feast: saucisson, rillettes, pasta salad, ewe's cheese and a Basque cake, and of course a bottle of red wine. Just like the old times!

After packing it all up, we all walk a few kilometers together, and review the events of the last few days. We meet them again in Ostabat, a meeting point on the trail as well. An examination of a sketch on my pilgrim's crédenciale shows one of the reasons why the scallop is a popular symbol of the pilgrimage. The ridges of the shell's exterior converge at the base in the way that three of the four main French routes converge right here at Ostabat. The route from Le Puy, the one we chose, the route from Vézelay, and the one from Arles.

Because it is raining, we don't spend much time in the village, but keep hiking toward Larceveau, where our hotel is located. After a quick installation, we visit the local museum featuring discoidal stones, an art piece of work that can be found in most of the Mediterranean countries. They are particularly abundant in the cemeteries of the Basque Country. They consist of a circular disc which overcomes one stone trapezoidal base. The disc is decorated with a Basque cross of geometric figures such as solar symbols, Christian and also vegetation symbols like trees. The deceased's name is rarely mentioned, but sometimes the family name is listed. The oldest are prior to the sixteenth century.

We enjoy an aperitif and dinner in the restaurant of the Hotel Trinquet. The conversation is animated with us sharing all the stories and adventures since the beginning of the week, and them filling us in on what is happening in the world these days. My mother and I have been morally protected from the tension and agitation growing in the western world in this fall of 2008. The financial markets are about to crash.

*****

This morning, we start our day with warm bread, just delivered from the bakery for the customers of the hotel! This is the last stretch to reach Saint Jean Pied-de-Port, the last town before ascending the Pyrenees and reaching Spain in Roncevaux, known as Roncesvalles in Spanish. The trail follows near and far the main road that leads to Saint Jean-Pied-de-Port. It is well done and not bothersome by any means. Not much is to report other than our immersion in the Basque landscape with the typical architecture of the Basque houses and villages, and the Pyrenees' chain, which is getting closer with each step.

Arriving in Saint-Jean-Pied-de-Port is magical. Saint Jean Pied-de-Port is a small town in the Basque region on the river Nive, about five miles from the Spanish border, nestled at the foot of the Pyrenees. Saint Jean Pied-de-Port is one of the traditional starting points of the Camino de Santiago for foreigners, referred to as the French Way or Camino Frances. Pied-de-Port means "foot of the pass," as the town sits at the base of the Roncevaux Pass through the Pyrenees. The French Way travels five hundred miles to Santiago. Other routes come from other areas in France to join the French

Way in Saint Jean Pied-de-Port, most notably the one from Le Puy which travels 460 miles. The Camino through France is far less utilized than the French Way.

Figure 26: St. Jean Pied-de-Port

The Nive River flows gently through Saint Jean Pied-de-Port.. For years, it has been an inspiration to artists such as Louis Dewis for his oil painting *The Bridge at Saint Jean Pied de Port.*

Arriving in the north by the chapel of the Madeleine, the pilgrims enter the upper town by the Porte Saint-Jacques, and then follow the road of Spain up to the bridge crossing over the Nive. In 1998, the Porte St-Jacques, the city gate, was added to the UNESCO World Heritage Sites as part of the sites along the Routes of Santiago de Compostela in France.

The cobblestone streets lead us to the center of town, where shops, hotels and restaurants are flourishing. On a side street, a traditional restaurant, not too fancy, offers an appealing menu. The inside, with small stone walls, wooden tables and chairs, gives off a mountainous atmosphere. We order large plates of sausage, piperade and local cheese. The *Piperade* is a typical Basque dish prepared with onion, green peppers, and tomatoes sautéed and flavored with red Espelette pepper. The colors coincidentally reflect the colors of the Basque flag—red, green and white. It may be served as a main course or as a side dish. Typical additions include egg, garlic or meats such as ham.

Our stomachs are full, our bodies warm and rested, and it is time to start climbing. My mother is a little scared, but truly excited. She takes off her backpack and gives it to her brother to travel by car, but I feel guilty and decide to keep mine at any cost. We have made the choice to sleep in Honto tonight, a hamlet three miles into the climb. We wanted to break it down if possible. After one week on the trail, we are warmed up, our endurance is at its peak, and our muscles are rock hard and ready to go. We are pleased to notice that this feared ascent is going a lot better than expected. We arrive in Honto without much suffering and almost pass it. The property, la ferme Ithurbia, offers an amazing sight. Overhanging the valley, it is leaning on the slope of the mountain. Unfortunately, the wet weather prevents us from enjoying the patio and terraces.

Our room has a balcony and is built on two levels, with a mezzanine where the second bed is located.

It is early enough in the day that we are able to drive back to Saint-Jean-Pied-de-Port for a thorough visit of the fortified bastion. Even though it is raining, we greatly enjoy visiting the famous town and buy a few food delicacies to bring home, now that we have a car to carry it all.

Back to our nest for the night, we settled in a cozy, semi-private living room and enjoy a bottle of wine bought in town for the occasion called '*Le Pèlerin*'. Dinner is served in a long room, where a long dining table has been set to accommodate all the pilgrims and guests, about twenty of us tonight. The discussion is mainly focused on the dreaded, mystical climb to Roncesvalles.

*****

Here we are, in front of the imposing mountain. We have to climb until we reach the pass to cross, and then start our descent toward Roncesvalles, a well-known monastery in Spain –the first sign of life after crossing the chain.

The mileage is imprecise and we can't quite tell if we are starting an eleven- or a thirteen-mile hike. It rained all night, and it is still raining when we depart. After an energetic breakfast, we hit the trail shortly before 8 a.m. We wear our ponchos over our backpacks and start climbing. As expected, it is a constant climb, with very few flat areas to catch our breath. The sky is threatening, with large fluffy clouds, hanging low, caught in the mountain tops, mostly white with dark grey tones.

Figure 27: The Sheep Leaving Their Summer Pasture to Return to the Village for Winter

We reach the high pastures quickly, and despite the effort required to keep up with the terrain, the feeling of freedom, the breathtaking sight, is uplifting. We are on top of the world, as high as the mountains around us; we are above 4,200 feet. Up here in the high pastures, the flocks of sheep have to leave their summer grazing pastures to return to the villages for the winter. Large flock trucks have made their way up here, and sheep dogs are gathering the sheep and cows for loading onto the trucks. Further yet, we see wild horses, a protected breed called Pottök. They are considered a prehistoric horse, rather short, with long and coarse hair. They might even be the descendants of horses that were painted in prehistoric caves.

Figure 28: Crossing the Pyrenees Mountains

Our pace is quite fast, and we pass many pilgrims during our ascent. It is a comforting thought to know so many are behind us. The sky is getting darker, the temperature is getting colder, and soon we are surprised to see snowflakes softly twirling down. We get out our scarves and gloves, and the snow flurries turn into snow showers, with the snow starting to accumulate on the ground. We reach the Bentarte pass at 4,750 feet. It is still snowing and we are cold, even though we are burning some energy.

Spain! We are in Spain! The signage is now changing. We say goodbye to our GR 65 and its red and white markings to follow large yellow arrows. The signage is particularly large in the mountains to avoid any unfortunate incidents during foggy days. People have lost their way in the past!

We can now begin the descent toward Roncesvalles, a stiff, uneven path through the forest covered with leaves. Above us, the thunder is loudly rolling through the mountains, bouncing from one to the other. We are now safe, but can't help feeling apprehensive for all the people we passed, still climbing in the storm.

Five hours non-stop to cross the Pyrenees chain due to the weather. Not bad! Alain and Danièle are watching for us at the bottom of the trail, anxious as they hear the thunder echoing in the valley.

The last step for the day is to get our credential stamped at the monastery. We grab lunch in a restaurant where only Spanish is spoken. Unbelievable, considering we just crossed the border, but a welcome reminder that we will need to brush up on our Spanish before next year.

As usual, it is hard to leave this world to return to the real world we live in, but our flight is leaving out of Biarritz tonight at 7:50 p.m. We are about one hour's drive away from Biarritz, a recreational city located on the Atlantic coast. The last stop before flying to Paris is the beach in Biarritz. We remove our hiking boots, put up our pants, and walk on the cool sand to the ocean. An hour ago, we were in the mountains, coping with snow showers, and now we are walking bare feet in the sand by the ocean. What a contrast!

Year Five

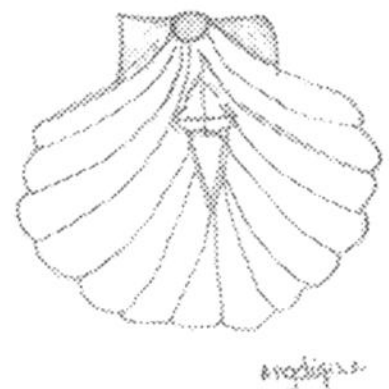

From Roncevaux to Santo Domingo de la Calzada
119 miles in 8 days

"For God gave us a spirit not of fear but of power and love and self-control."
2 Timothy 1:7

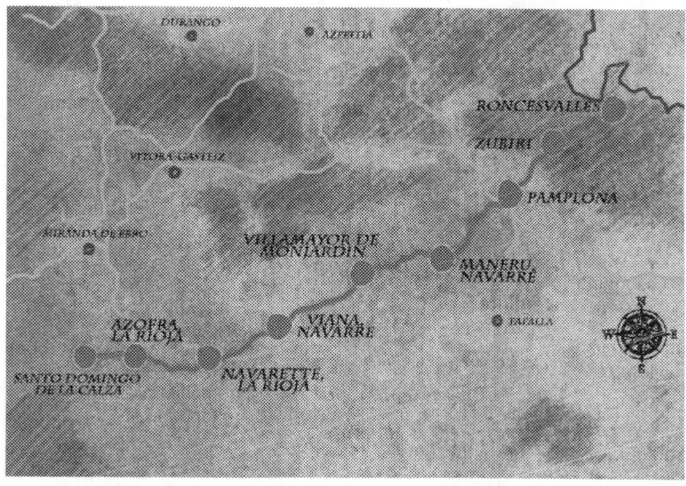

September has come again, and we are looking forward to start our fifth year hiking the trail. El Camino is waiting for us to return. We travel back to Biarritz on a bright and early flight, and have breakfast at the airport. Chez Paul is never a disappointment, though. We are in Paris after all, where food is rarely neglected.

Biarritz, the European surfing spot, is overcast when we arrive. Our taxi driver, booked from Paris, is waiting for us in the arrival hall. We are on our way to Roncevaux, through the luxuriant vegetation of the Basque countryside. For merely one hour and a half, we discuss with vivid interest the political and cultural aspects of this strong region; a bit rebellious, even the delicate subject of Francoism in France and Spain.

The climb to Roncevaux is a reminder of what we climbed last year on foot. We ascend the narrow, winding road in the Pyrenees, crossing the border through a thick fog, or as we say in French, *un brouillard à couper au couteau,* so thick of a fog you need a knife to cut it.

Figure 29: Mountainous Trail

We wave goodbye to our chauffeur and look at each other with a déjà vu sensation. It is only 10:30 a.m., and we have thirteen and a half miles to cover for this first adjusting day. The air is crisp and cool up here.

The first Spanish village we cross is Burguete. A small village, built in length, it is lined with typical Basque houses offering pretty blazoned façades from the twelfth century. The village is quiet and there is no one to be seen. Our next stop is Espinal, another small mountainous village where we find an open café. A ham and cheese omelet, Spanish style, rustic and filling, satisfies our appetite.

The afternoon is very pleasant and offers beautiful scenery of the countryside of Navarra. We cross the village of Viscarret, with large family homes decorated with blazons, and Lintzoain. The alpine terrain brings a variety of uphill and downhill rocky trails, narrow passages, fords over streams, and gates to open and shut in the high pastures where livestock spend the summer. In a nutshell, the mind as well as the eye, is constantly aroused by the beauty of the surrounding mountains.

We are perched all day at a rather high altitude, ranging from 1,600 feet to 3,000 feet. The air is cooler, but mild enough that we can hike in a t-shirt. Four hours later, and after a steep, broken slope, we enter the town of Zubiri, our night stage. The medieval bridge crossing the Arga River welcomes travelers to this remote town in the Pyrenees.

The town is small in size and a stopping point for many pilgrims. Backpacks and hiking boots for some, flip flops and casual clothes for others, reveal who is who. We are in hiking land. We meander through the streets until we find a small hotel, the hosteria de Zubiri, where only one, last room is available. The day has been long. We got up at 4:30 a.m. in Paris, still coping with jet lag, traveled to the south, caught a lengthy cab ride, and hiked over thirteen miles. Comfort sounds appropriate for this first night, and a hotel will do the trick.

After a furtive tour of the town, not by choice but limited by its size, we return to the hotel for dinner. Tired and eager to get to bed, we inquire about eating dinner at the front desk since there is not much activity in the dining room. We are confronted with a new concept that did not occur to us: we are now in Spanish land and must observe the cultural differences. Spaniards eat much later than French people, which means that they won't serve us any earlier than 8:30 p.m., considered a favor since they usually don't eat before 9:30 p.m. Do like Spaniards in Spain is our new motto.

*****

This morning we opt for a late start, around 8:15 a.m., since we decided to stop in Pamplona, only fourteen miles away, to spend the night and explore this well-known city. Our plan has changed. Even though we had well-studied the itinerary from Paris and Green Bay in the previous months, we have been advised last night at dinner by our table neighbors, two charming men from Laval in Brittany, to cut short our stage tomorrow and remain in Pamplona for an evening. Convinced, we voted for the switch of itinerary.

We leave Zubiri, following a small shady trail which leads to an unexpected panoramic view of a factory of meerschaum, a natural silicate of magnesium. The decor is surprisingly colorless and bare, where only the factory seems alive. We are grateful to reconnect with nature shortly after, where trees and shade are present again.

We make our way to Larrasona after an hour, and enter the village through a beautiful medieval bridge, El Puente de los Bandidos. The village is deserted. This is now becoming a trend that we have noticed. The villages are all very calm, almost uninhabited during the day. It is too hot—the shades are shut, the youngsters are gone to work and the elders are staying in, hiding from the heat. Nevertheless, when the heat fades away, we notice the villages' squares fill up with locals.

Iroz, a few miles further, makes a perfect halt spot for us. We find a unique stone bench, built up on two levels, by the church in the center of the village. Except for a couple of pilgrims walking by, there is not a soul in sight except for a sad-looking cat, skinny and starved. We feel sorry for him and share our snack with him, hoping he will not get sick from all this abundance of food. Prosciutto, Pyrenees cheese and grapes. He devours everything.

Zabaldika, another small village on the way, is only six miles away from Pamplona. Only twenty-nine inhabitants live in just eight homes. The houses are built out of carved stones, representing the typical architecture from the seventeenth and eighteenth centuries. Upon our arrival, an older woman, a sister of the Sacred Heart, welcomes us in French. Her French is quite good, and she invites us to visit the church. She unlocks the door of this thirteenth-century church, turns on some light and music, and we proceed to enter this haven. She hands us a typed sheet, all in French, describing the church in details. We browse around and exchange a few words and many smiles with our host. We feel renewed.

Figure 30: Signage to Follow in Spain

We resume our journey at one o'clock in the afternoon. The sun is high in the sky and scorching hot. With this heat, it is painful to reach the next point. This portion of the trail, a little bit dreaded from previous readings is actually very pleasant. Even though the RN 135, the main road that leads to Pamplona, is always somewhat in sight, the trail is never too close, a bit elevated, and surrounded by vegetation.

The entrance of Villava, a five-arch medieval bridge, opens into a long street that we take on the left. Homes, built on two or three floors, touch each other to make a continuous wall on one side of the street. Sprays of bright-colored flowers hang from balconies. On the other side is something less common: barricades built out of raw wood, thick and tall, border the length of the street. There are no sidewalks, just a paved street, sort of tunneled in.

"What is that?" I throw out there, hoping for an answer. Looking at my mom's puzzled face, I conclude she is asking herself the same question.

Approaching Pamplona, we arrive from the north side of the city, crossing the Magdalena Bridge over the Rio Arga. We then follow the ramparts that lead to the Porte de France, a drawbridge door.

Disconnected from the real world, our first sight of Pamplona is disturbing. The winding street, lined with two- and three story buildings, is narrow and not paved, covered with compacted dirt. Hundreds of people of all ages are in the street, some sitting on the ground, others leaning against the walls, all speaking loudly, laughing obnoxiously and drinking beer. We are standing out in the middle of this crowd with our tired air, hiking boots and large backpacks, but no one seems to care. They are accustomed to pilgrims arriving daily to their city.

It is only early afternoon, and this is not a common sight. We picked a good day you may say! We find out that today is a special day in Pamplona. They are celebrating a small version of la Feria de la San Fermin, which usually takes place in July. This one is dedicated to the children. There is no danger—no young cows will be released wildly in the streets; just fun and laughter. We now look back and understand the barricades in Villava and the dirt road entering Pamplona. It all makes sense. We are in the land of corridas.

The origin of the fiesta of San Fermín goes back to the Middle Ages and is related to three celebrations: Religious ceremonies in honour of San Fermín, which intensified from the twelfth century onward, trade fairs and bullfights, which were first documented in the fourteenth century.

Much of the worldwide fame of the Sanfermines is due to the references made by Ernest Hemingway in his articles as a reporter and his novel, *The Sun Also Rises*, known as *Fiesta* in the Spanish-speaking world.

The future Nobel Prize winner first visited Pamplona on July 6, 1923, accompanied by his wife, Hadley Richardson. The Sanfermines made such an impression on him that he returned on several occasions. During his visits to Pamplona, he usually stayed at the Hotel La Perla in the Plaza del Castillo. It was quite common to see him on the cafe terraces of the Plaza del Castillo, running the bulls or avoiding the young bulls in the bull ring. These frisky animals gave him quite a few scary moments! A great admirer of the corrida and bullfighters, Hemingway never missed a bullfight. He had a taste for the traditional dishes of the Navarrese cuisine and was a regular in restaurants and bars such as Casa Marceliano.

We find our hotel for the night on Plaza Virgen, and after a late lunch on a busy square, under shady trees, we are ready to explore. We feel light as a feather without backpacks or heavy hiking boots. Pamplona is definitely worth the detour. We would have missed out if we had to continue to the next town, visiting Pamplona like hikers rather than tourists. Pampelona surely deserves a half day of our time to breathe in its heart and soul.

With a population of nearly 200,000, the capital of the region of Navarra has a beautiful medieval city center. We spend the afternoon meandering through the park, the city's main square, winding streets, El Corte Ingles, a department store, the citadel, the ramparts and the cathedral, which unfortunately is closed for the rest of the day.

We walk through narrow, animated streets, lined with tapas bars as we head toward la Plaza del Castillo, where Hemingway used to dine. It is too early to eat dinner, but tapas are offered all day long, as well as small portion dishes. The Plaza del Castillo, a very large square, is surrounded by buildings, where locals and tourists pack the cafes and their terraces. We dine on a small plate of Paella Mixta, followed by a plate of ewe's milk cheese, along with a glass of Sangria.

Paella Mixta

Serves: 4-6

Ingredients:

- 1 tsp. saffron
- 2 tsp. paprika
- 2 medium onions, chopped
- 2 red bell peppers, chopped
- 2 pounds tomatoes, chopped
- 4 garlic cloves, chopped
- 3 chicken thighs, skinned and cut into 2 inch pieces, seasoned with salt and pepper
- 12 large raw shrimp, peeled
- 12 mussels (or clams)
- 1 lb. Spanish cooking chorizo, cut into 1 inch pieces
- 8 Tb. olive oil
- Sea salt and pepper
- 2 cups rice
- 6 cups chicken broth
- Lemon wedges

Method:

Combine the chicken broth, paprika and saffron in a covered pot and cook over medium heat for five minutes.

In a paella pan, add 2 Tb. of olive oil and brown the chicken and the chorizo. Remove.

Add the remaining olive oil and cook the onions over medium heat. Add the bell peppers and cook for a few minutes. Add the tomatoes and garlic and simmer until they have a sauce-like appearance. Salt and pepper to taste.

Add the rice and stir until the rice is covered with the tomato mixture. Add chicken and chorizo pieces. Then slowly add the broth to the paella pan. Stir the rice mixture around until it is evenly distributed throughout the pan. Important - do not stir after this point.

Simmer for about ten minutes, then place the shrimp and shellfish into the pan. Simmer until all the broth has been absorbed adding extra liquid if needed. Remove from heat, cover with foil and let stand for another 10 minutes.

Garnish with lemon wedges.

The history of sangria is pretty straightforward. Over 2,000 years ago, the Romans made their way through the Iberian Peninsula and planted vineyards along the way. As water at that time was considered unsafe for drinking, it was common to fortify it with alcohol to kill off any bacteria. The first sangrias, whose name comes from *sangre*, or blood, and refers to its dark color, were likely heavily watered down mixes of wine, water, and herbs and spices. They would add anything to kill off the bacteria in the water and disguise the bad to mediocre table wine. The easiest way to think of modern day sangria is as a wine punch, often involving fruit and other alcohols. But it is important to note that there is no standard recipe in Spain.

The streets are becoming fuller, the voices are rising, and the Spaniards are coming out. The night ends for us while starting for others, with unexpected fireworks for the Fiesta, before heading back to our hotel. The night is a bit lively, and it is hard to get a good night's sleep. Late into the night, the city pours out its heated crowd noises. What a treat! Pamplona was indeed a good choice, a must-see in Spain.

*****

Figure 31: Iron Sculpture of Pilgrims

Today is a big day. We have to make up for the mileage we shortened yesterday. Breakfast early, and after one last stop at the *panaderia*, we say goodbye to Pamplona. The road is busy with other pilgrims, a first since our start this year. It is fun to people watch and start knowing who is who on the trail. A thick fog accompanies us until mid-morning, giving way to a deep blue sky and a bright hot sun.

Corn fields go on endlessly toward a massive mountainous range, which crest is planted with a forest of white, lengthy, modern wind-powered mills.

We take our 11 o'clock break in Zariquiegui near the church, resting before ascending the steep slope to the Sierra del Perdon peak. At the top, the view is breathtaking. Behind us, the plain of Pamplona extends all the way to the Pyrenees, which allows one last look at the chain. In front of us lays the valley of Valdizarbe. We stop a moment to admire the scenery, as well as a group of pilgrims, riding horses, donkeys and walking, all silhouettes carved in rusty-color metal sheets, pointing the way for real pilgrims. We can't resist posing for the cliché picture, walking among them.

On our way down, toward Uterga, the vegetation changes. Colchicums cover the ground. Their delicate purple color stands out, while the way they grow is unique. They just seem to pop out of the ground, with no leaf or stem underneath. We also discover the beginning of the *maquis*, or scrubland, almond trees, vineyards and olive trees. We have left the high mountain to find a milder climate in which this vegetation flourishes. The almonds are ready, and we are delighted to pick some right from the trees and stuff our pockets for later snacks.

This part of the day is memorable for the lack of shade. We finally arrive in Uterga, thirsty. A large glass of Perrier topped with orange juice is so refreshing. Everyone at the *albergue* is eating lunch, but we are overheated and not hungry. We decide to leave them all behind and set off toward the next village.

We cross asparagus fields, something I had never seen before. Obanos, the next village, is our next stop. Again, we are thirsty and this time up for some munchies. I go inside to see what is available. Today is Sunday, and some *Pintxos*, the local term for tapas, are served all day for locals. Halved hard boiled eggs, covered with two anchovies and topped with an olive is one example. Filled with good food, we resume our expedition toward Puenta La Reina.

Figure 32: Tapas, or Pintxos

Puente la Reina, a medieval town known as "the crossroads of the ways," is where the two main routes on the Pilgrim's Way to Santiago de Compostela converge. It is also the official start of the Camino Frances, different from the Camino Del Norte, the coastal northern route or the Via de la Plata, coming from Seville.

Near the albergue, pilgrims sit on the ground against the wall, backpacks lying next to them, as they wait in line for the albergue to open and hope to get a bed for the night. In case they don't have enough beds, a few mattresses will be available to lie on the floor between beds or in the hallways. There are only three or four showers for the whole place. A massive rush takes place when the doors open midafternoon—it is cheap and only for pilgrims. One must show pilgrimage stamped papers to enter and benefit from the low rate.

As we amble along the streets, we notice opened maroon gates lining the main street, blocking access to side roads. Further along, we see carriage entrance-style doors that still have metal gates protecting the wood. We missed it; just like in Pamplona, the fiesta took place here yesterday, only bulls were part of it.

Too early to stop, we continue and cross the six-arch bridge to exit the town. Maneru is only three miles away. Asparagus fields and red pimientos, a small sweet pepper, are growing everywhere. The last couple of miles are miserable; we are climbing nonstop in the burning sun, where no shade can relieve us. Arriving at the top, we find the casa rural, Isabel, where we are staying.

With bright red cheeks, we enter the rejuvenating garden, hidden behind large, private wooden doors. The hostess welcomes us, a bit concerned at our sight. We remove our backpacks and ask for a *clarita*, a beer cut with Sprite. To our surprise, she refuses and brings us water instead, claiming that we need to recover before having a clarita. Amused, we drink our water and thank her, proceed to remove our shoes, and get acquainted with our bedrooms and such. The garden is a haven after this hot day. Lots of trees, green grass, flowers and areas to rest. No one else is staying here tonight, so the place is ours! Since the sun is still out, we decide to wash a few items and hang them outside to dry in the sun.

A little stroll in town later on, and we are back to the casa to enjoy a homemade peregrinos menu composed of vegetable soup, *bacalao*, salad, cheese, yogurt, apples, and of course, almonds collected in our pockets.

*****

After breakfast at the casa, we take along tomatoes and grapes from the garden for the picnic later today. The sun is just peaking over the hills, and we can see the next village, Cirauqui, perched on top of a hill.

We pass through and exit crossing a Roman bridge leading to the remains of a Via Romana in pretty good shape, heading to Lorca. We arrive mid-morning, just in time to take our morning break at the albergue in the middle of the village. Hungry, I order a sandwich made with *lomo* and mild *pimientos*. Our appetite has now evolved with the required daily effort. More food with more miles. Further, Villatuerta, a modern town surrounded by numerous industries, is not worth mentioning except for its beautiful church and medieval bridge.

We become uneasy at the sight of a handwritten message along the road for all pilgrims and hikers to see, warning that we are now entering the Basque country. We wonder if we are welcomed.

We reach Estella, located on the borders of the Rio Ega. Near the beautiful church Santo Sepulcro, a little old lady starts conversing with us in Spanish about her trifles. She shares her concerns about the heat and how tired she is from her walk back from the cemetery. Now, you have to realize that over here all the grandmas and grandpas walk everywhere, with or without a cane, at their own pace, regardless of the weather. Their endurance is amazing when you consider the hills they have to climb daily just to get groceries or visit their lost ones at the cemetery.

Motivated to find a cool spot near the rio for a relaxing lunch, we buy groceries and start our quest for the perfect place. The word perfect quickly disappears. Nothing! We are tired, hot, hungry, but there is nothing in sight; just sidewalks and city materials. We have to wait for Ayegui, a suburb at the exit of Estella, to find a bench, a tree and a triangle of grass. While unsatisfied, we settled for it.

September is grape-harvesting season. The vineyards are busy with workers and machines, picking and loading grapes to become the cherished liquid. We make the traditional stop at Irache, a monastery known for its wine fountain, Bodegas Irache. A taste, a picture are enough. The wine is a little green.

A mile and a half to climb to end the day. Villamayor de Monjardin is at the top. Without a reservation, we have the advantage of choosing our bed tonight. However, the village, perched on a small hill, is tiny and offers only two lodging options. The first one we go to is listed as privately owned and offers rooms with sixteen guests in each, with only two top bunk beds left. I vote this one out, picturing myself trying to climb down in the middle of the night for a bathroom break.

The second lodging is supported by the parish and offers a roof to all. One large room is organized with a large type of wood banquette in a U-shape, where mattresses are set next to each other all the way around the room. Another small room, already full, has a few bunk beds jammed in there. No blankets or pillows are handed out, just a mattress and access to two bathrooms and two showers, for twenty people in all. The bathrooms, made out of thin plywood, are central, and all sound effects audible by all, are hard to ignore. Charming!

Figure 33: Our Mattresses in Villa Major de Monjardin

Our choice is made—we are going with option number two. We are given a warm welcome, along with a cup of tea and a friendly conversation. We get our sleeping bags out, blow up our inflatable pillows, and get our PJs ready. With our backpacks on the floor at the end of the mattress, we are set for a shower.

After showering, doing a little laundry, hanging our socks and underwear in a little garden behind the church among men's and women's underpants, we converge toward the one and only place to eat in town. It is on the square facing the *pelota* court, and is well-attended with the whole village, mostly pilgrims, wanting to eat.

"Hola," I address the innkeeper. "We would like to eat dinner here tonight."

"No problem! Please come back for 7 p.m." he replies.

We sit outside at a table on the square and order an aperitif. Asking the waiter for a local drink, he brings out two glasses of *Pacharan*, a concoction made of anise and sloe, dark in color, with a unique strong flavor, our new drink of the week.

Figure 34: Drying Laundry Behind the Church

At 7 p.m., we all gather in the restaurant and form a long table of mixed nationalities. We converse about our different stages and individual encounters while eating a hearty and delicious meal. Then it's time to return to our "communal room" for the night, where the light is officially out at 10:00 p.m. sharp.

*****

In spite of the precarious conditions, we sleep relatively soundly, apart from the few middle-of-the-night toilet flushes and early risers leaving at dark around 5 a.m. Breakfast is a feast. We are introduced to what is called pilgrim's fuel. It is a delicious slice of toasted country bread, smothered with a homemade mixture of crushed sun-ripened tomatoes, oregano, olive oil and salt.

The morning is enjoyable, with trails winding through vast stretches of cultivated fields on rolling hills, with vivid colors changing from yellows to oranges to golden tones, depending on the sun angle. The sky is hazy, the sun is hot, and there is no shade anywhere. First blister!

Three hours nonstop to reach Los Arcos. We are glad to see a bit of civilization. The first impression, as we approach, is disappointing. There is a sense of poverty, along with an overly rural aspect. The main part of the town is hidden behind a hill. As we make our way to the inner part of the town, we discover that many streets are torn apart and in the process of being rehabilitated. Los Arcos has numerous large and beautiful buildings.

Figure 35: Enjoying my new Spanish Hat, Bought at an Outdoor Market

We stumble onto a market in the central square, where we decide to invest in a hat to protect us from the sun and heat. The choices are minimal and we have to settle for unattractive and rather silly floral print hats, a pink one for me and the same in aqua blue for my mother. Across from the market, a café terrace is calling us. We sit down and order an omelet, made with potatoes and vegetables.

Glad to have purchased our new, bright and noticeable hats, we put them to good use right away on our way to Sansol. The road is deadly, mainly straight, with a sad tree every few miles offering a mere area of shade on the wrong side of the trail. There is no water, no livestock, no people; just us two and the sun. Sansol is in sight, at the top of a hill, which finishes us. Blushed, wet and tired, we are welcomed by a photographer right at the top of the hill who is shooting pictures of the pitiful pilgrims arriving sparingly, and then posting them on the internet.

Torres del Rio, the next village, is just a bit further away. We manage to walk there to stop for our lunch. Stopping too early would jeopardize the possibility of arriving at a decent hour in Viana tonight. We still have almost seven miles to reach Viana and no reservation made for sleeping. We end up shopping for lunch at the *tienda* and find a lonely bench in total shade near a thick stone wall. Some pilgrims have reached their final destination and are already in their flip flops, reading a book on a shady church step in the village.

It is very tempting to cave in and stop here, but we are determined to sleep in Viana tonight. So after one hour of well-deserved rest, we put our shoes back on, muster all of our courage, and start the last leg of the day. Two and half hours later, a view of tall public housing types of buildings surrounding a town announces Viana. We ignore the new part of town and climb –yes, there is always a little bit of hidden energy left to find the adequate, pleasing location—to reach the "pueblo" to the plaza de los Fueros.

Eager to make a noticeable contrast with last night, we treat ourselves to a palace for the night. A three-star hotel, although a bit luxurious for dirty hikers, will be a great revenge over last night. Our second excuse is that today, September 29, is the celebration of Saint Michel.

Tonight we demand to see another menu than the *peregrinos* menu for €9. The waiter suggests the menu special for €16.50 and nothing more extravagant. Peregrinos remain peregrinos.

Today was our last day in the Comunidad, or region, de Navarra. Tomorrow, we will enter the Comunidad de la Rioja, known internationally for its good wines.

*****

We leave Viana in the morning going west and find the explanation to the large amount of public housing units. A large Kraft factory has been built here on the outskirts of the town. This also answers questions we had at dinner last night, when hearing a handful of American businessmen having dinner a few tables down. American businessmen in Viana? Really? Yes, really. Viana, this remote little town, is known to the American business world.

La Rioja is a very fertile part of Spain and has an abundant supply of water due to the seven major rivers that flow through it. Small in size, the province is very rich in natural resources. Its main economy is wine production and its related industries. There has been a tradition of wine harvesting in this region of Spain since the Phoenicians. Literally the entire region is covered with vineyards, from tiny family owned and operated bodegas to massive industrial producers.

Vineyards are becoming more prominent, small and large, hilly and flat, which can require handpicking, as we notice here and there.

Logrono, the capital of La Rioja, is a major city, and as expected, the arrival is long—about three miles—and very industrial. To enter Logrono, we cross a seven-arch bridge over the Ebro River. Many parts of the old town are being renovated. Sometimes only the façade is conserved, while the whole building is demolished. The Rua Vieja leads to the Santiago El Real church, hosting a magnificent retable dedicated to St. James.

The noise, car exhaust, and commotion are all disturbing. Only four days away from our daily life, and already our minds and bodies have adjusted to a more serene way of life. We have lunch on the terrace of a café in the center of town and order *tostas* – a slice of toasted bread covered with tomato sauce, olive oil, cheese and Serrano ham. We look out of place amongst all these office workers, nicely dressed, during their lunch hour. But they don't even seem to notice us.

The exit of Logrono is unsightly but rapid. Quickly we enter the Parque de la Grajera bordering a wide water stretch, a three-mile-long athletic track shared by bikers, walkers and runners. It has only been a little over an hour since we left the café in Logrono, but we can't resist stopping at the terrace of a restaurant with a lake view. Our table, covered with a white and blue checkered table cloth, sits halfway in the shade and faces the lake. We order a whole meal of spaghetti and tomato sauce, salad and a *clarita*. Stuffed but content, we head out for Navarette.

A wire fence bordering the trail keeps hikers from wandering off toward the highway that's slightly downward to our right. In the distance, we distinguish a unique catchy artwork on the fence: pilgrims have started a new trend to show their passage. With sticks only, peeled or weathered, collected on the trail, they have intertwined their findings to create crosses in the wire fence. Covering a long section of this part of the trail, it keeps our minds occupied watching all the artistic creations. It is a testimonial of people's faith and helps us forget about the major highway running parallel to the trail below.

Another interesting sight, typical to the region, is perched on top of a bare hill, meant to be seen from far away, whether walking, biking or on the highway. A massive, brown metal, cut-out bull is standing there, reminding all that we are in the land of bull runs and bull fights. Moreover, to point out that this is indeed a bull and not a cow, his private parts are highlighted with a vibrant red paint. A little bit of Spanish humor!

We arrive in Navarette around four in the afternoon, early enough to look for lodging. We find a small hotel in the old part of town in the Alta Mayor Calle. The paved street encircles the village and is bordered by two- or three-story-high colorful constructions. The village is quiet yet and we go on to visit it, starting with the monumental church of the Ascension from the sixteenth century, with its three naves, home to a valuable seventeenth-century Baroque altarpiece.

*****

With only a basic and light breakfast from the sleepy bar in the hotel, we leave under a cloudy sky. A stop at the *panaderia* down the road to load up on sugary morning pastries completes the frugal meal.

The largely agricultural region is a succession of low, rolling hills and valleys where vineyards grow indefinitely. The trail is never too far from the RN20, the major road leading to Santiago, which was "the" original trail to Santiago. The trail has been redrawn by its side, staying as truthful as possible to the original path and trying to make it as pleasant as possible.

During a little pause on the edge of a vineyard, sharing hard-boiled eggs, cheese and handpicked walnuts, we are rushed to get back to work by a few drops of rain, a first since we are in Spain. We inaugurate our brand new ponchos, with arms, zippered all the way down, a large hump in the back to accommodate the backpack and an adjustable fitted hood, replacing our torn ponchos destroyed last year in the Pyrenees while coping with snow, wind and cold temperatures.

The day goes by watching the grape harvesting, an intense, timely process, more or less industrial depending on the shapes and sizes of the lots.

Najera, that we nicknamed rat hole, is a town of little interest with grey stones, busy streets and daily workers in line waiting to be hired. Initially we planned to stay here for the night, but we're glad that our itinerary has changed. We find a lovely, rather elegant restaurant for lunch, on a small quiet square away from the busy and sad-looking streets. Daringly, we take our chances and enter with our muddy hiking boots and cumbersome backpacks.

Figure 36: Pulpo Gallego

A corner round table is appointed to us, which allows us to easily dispose of our backpacks and hiking sticks. The place is filled with businessmen and women on lunch. We catch their eye, exchange a couple of smiles, and everyone resumes their conversations. Our meal is excellent, fancy, local and a step up from our daily, "mandatory" peregrinos menu. We discover the *pulpo gallego*, a dish in which octopus is served cut in thin slices, all arranged flat on a plate, covered with colorful orange spices, oil and served warm. Delicious!

Our goal is to reach Azofra for the night, a small agricultural village where a public albergue offers many beds, according to our book.

Upon arriving, we stop in front of a small, open-style shop. We are intrigued by an archaic-looking machine standing in the middle of the room that peels off almonds. Removing the thick, velvety, greenish shell, it leaves the almond all clean in its hard, tan shell. The workers are amused by our sense of curiosity and hand us a handful of almonds.

The albergue, located a bit further and off to the right of the main strip, has been built to accommodate the many pilgrims that cross this region. It is clean and the host is welcoming.

The hikers' laundry, drying at the entrance of the yard, welcomes everyone and announces the type of guests residing here tonight. The building is worth a note of description. Built on three stories, this large concrete building block, dropped from nowhere in the middle of this tiny rural village, can accommodate up to sixty pilgrims in semi-private rooms for two. It is a definite step up from our mattress night in Villamayor.

Reaching our floor, the hallway leads to a series of small closet doors to our right and a set of windows to our left. The walls are made of raw plywood and the doors don't have a key. Each door, numbered to its right–ours is eighteen–opens up to a closet. You could compare it to a train compartment, with two couchettes arranged with red plaid covers, each labeled with letter A or B.

Once the doors closed, we discover two small individual spaces at the head of our beds where we can set our personal belongings. The luxury is that we have a sliding door that opens up to a ledge, large enough to set our shoes to air out during the night, with a permanent metal shade keeping the rooms cool but blocking the view. The floor, tiled in large brownish squares, has the merit of being clean.

The bathrooms, down the hall, mixed, have sinks, showers that do not lock and toilets. We get in line for the showers in the long hallway and wait for our turn while holding our bathroom essentials and a traveling-size towel. Halfway through my shower, the door cracks open.

"Someone's here," I shout in my shaky Spanish, thinking of the mixed bathroom situation. I hear no answer, but thankfully the door slowly shuts. Relieved, I pursue, but this incident has undeniably shortened my indulging shower as I'm worried it might happen again.

Leaving our prison-style lodging while acknowledging the rather practical concept, we go about exploring the village. In the main strip, a café with a few tables outside makes the perfect spot for an aperitif. After unsuccessfully trying to open up our almonds with rocks, the sympathetic owner brings us a nutcracker. Eating, drinking and writing our diary, we now stare at the end of the road from our lookout post, scanning the horizon in wait of the last hikers of the day.

After a visit of the church, led by an old lady, we find the bar restaurant Camino de Santiago for dinner, where a copious meal is served in a colorful dining room.

*****

Friday is already here! This week has gone by so fast. The trails this morning look like Russian mountains, a continuation of rolling hills running for miles. In Ciruena, the marking of the trail is uncertain, so we guess a bit, taking left or right turns, through this modern, newly built town. After a snack at the café bar in Ciruena, a little bit further, we notice hikers in the distance on a trail west of us and discover that the trail, still not so well marked, does not come through here. Brave and determined, we hike *hors-piste*, crossing ploughed fields, where the coarse, thick soil sticks to our feet and reaches up to the middle of our hiking boots. The uneven and uphill terrain, along with the weight of the backpack, makes it twice as hard to move forward. Inching our way with each step toward the trail of people we see in the distance, we ask each other, "What did we miss?"

Santo Domingo de la Calzada, our last stop for this year, appears at the right time. Struggling with a sore knee, my mother's pace has slowed down slightly, and while suffering quietly, she is glad to see the sign announcing Santo Domingo.

Rich in history, the town is home to a cathedral that hosts a "gallincro" or hen house, a symbol that reminds all about a miracle which took place here in the fourteenth century. The story relates the misadventure of a couple of pilgrims, accompanied by their son, Hugonell, who had stopped at an inn for the night. A waitress, angry at their son for not being her lover for a night, took revenge by placing a silver cup in his belongings and denouncing him. Judged and hung, the son's parents left, heartbroken. Upon their return from Santiago, where they prayed to St. James, they heard the voice of their son from the gallows—their beloved son is not dead! Overjoyed, they ran to the judge, who was eating a rooster and a hen, reporting the great news. To which the judge replied: "If your son is alive, this hen and rooster will start dancing in my plate." The rooster sang and the hen cackled, and the stupefied judge requested the immediate release of the son. Since then, a rooster and a hen, replaced every twenty days, live in a hen house in the cathedral in memory of the innocent son.

Midafternoon, a cab takes us to Burgos, a city located ahead of our actual position only thirty-seven miles away. The main train station, which is a way out of the center of town, has no checkroom. It is only 4 p.m. and our train is leaving late this evening, so we would like to get rid of our backpacks for a while. The taxi takes us to the bus station, which to his belief still has lockers, a rare thing nowadays. The station is right in the center of town, which is much more convenient for us to spend the next few hours.

Burgos still preserves important vestiges of its medieval splendor. The city, which was the capital of the unified kingdom of Castilla-Leon for five centuries, boasts a masterpiece of Spanish Gothic architecture; the cathedral of Burgos, declared World Heritage. Named *Catedral de Santa María*, it is notable for its vast size, white tones, magnificent Gothic architecture, and unique history. Built over several centuries, the first phase of construction took place between 1221 and 1293, with further embellishments made toward the middle of the fifteenth century.

The marvelous town gate Arco de Santa Maria gives way to the square where the cathedral is situated. The center of Burgos, the old town, is very well preserved and surrounded by ramparts.

We board the touristic train stationed by the cathedral and embark on a tour of Burgos, which takes us to a high point from where there is a view of the city worth the detour.

Since the trail crosses Burgos, we make mental notes for next year; almost three miles east to west, a good hour to cross this urban area.

Too early for dinner, per Spanish standards, we end up in a wine bar on the old square and relax while people watching. We end our day with dinner in a restaurant facing the cathedral, where we can order from a regular menu that inevitably is much more pricy compared to the traditional peregrinos menu.

We head back to the bus station to pick up our backpacks and load them up one more time. We hop in a taxi going in the direction of the train station, where the train in provenance of Madrid heading for Paris overnight is delayed by a long half hour, unheard of for a train. It is dark and late, and many people are waiting on the outdoor platform. Tired and a bit annoyed, we are glad to see the train enter the station at 10:45 p.m.

Our night, in a cabin of four couchettes, is shared with two ladies, not speaking French or much English either, but hikers, too. We all crawl in bed for a few hours of rest. We arrive on time in Paris Austerlitz train station the next morning despite the late departure from Burgos.

Looking back at this first year in Spain, we notice two aspects that we had to adjust to: we can rarely stop in nature for lunch or other mini breaks; and the pilgrims are more tunneled on the trails, preventing them from sitting in fields or other private properties. For the most part, stops have to be made in bars and restaurants. Also, pilgrims are concerned about finding a bed at night and often start their hiking day much earlier, many times in the dark, using a headlight, to arrive early at the albergue. They then spend their afternoon doing their laundry, reading and socializing.

Year Six

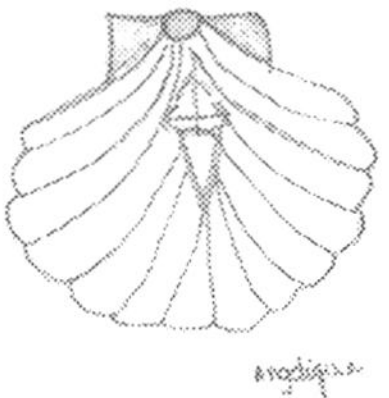

From Santo Domingo de la Calzada to Sahagun
127 miles in 7 days

"Fear not, for I am with you; be not dismayed, for I am your God; I will strengthen you, I will help you, I will uphold you with my righteous right hand."

Isaiah 41:10

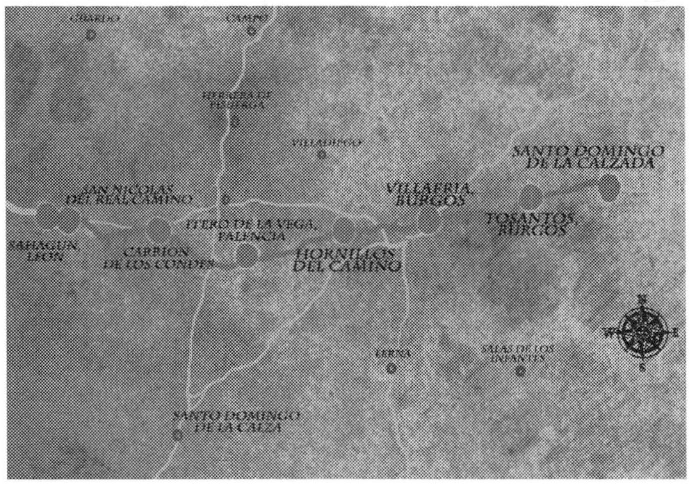

Heading back to Burgos this September, we have found a night hotel train from Gare d'Austerlitz, on the left bank of Paris, straight to Burgos. I arrive from Green Bay on Thursday morning, and our train is scheduled to leave at 7:47 p.m.

France is shaken by a national strike, triggered by complaints about new laws affecting retirement plans, which has some repercussion on the train system. We're pretty confident that our international train won't be affected by the strike, but we call the station to double check. It's a good thing we do, because we find out that even though it is an international train, it has been cancelled. Caught off guard, we hurry to secure another cabin-room on the next train. The next train does not leave until tomorrow night, since it also is a night train. Our time is now shortened since my return flight to the US is scheduled in a week. We are bummed.

Let's be optimistic. One day at home won't hurt, and the delay allows more time to see my dad, grandma and cousins, and shop and enjoy my home town. And realistically, some people would beg to spend a day in Paris, so whining sounds inappropriate.

Downtown Paris, still dealing with strikes, is packed on a Friday night. The traffic is so bad that we debate getting out of the car and taking the metro to the station. Two hours later, we get out of the car, kiss my dad goodbye, and go look for our Elipsos hotel train.

We board on time, find our private cabin, and get settled. The cabin for two is set up with two captain's chairs next to each other, a little bathroom with a shower, toilet and sink, but no beds.

Around dinner time, we leave our cabin and head to the restaurant car, where a dressed table for two by the window is reserved for us. The restaurant is full and the atmosphere is warm, with red and white tones radiating from the linens and table decorations. The slight waddling we experience as we motion toward our table reminds us that we are in a train. We choose the gourmet menu and enjoy a great evening, catching up on family stories.

Returning to our cabin a couple of hours later, we find our room transformed by the train maids, who created space for two spacious bunk beds.

My sleep is not so sound with the time change, and I awake in the middle of the night to notice the train is not moving. I open the curtains to peek outside and distinguish a building in the near distance, an industrial type of building, among many tracks. We are at the French-Spanish border near Biarritz in the southwest of France, and it is pouring out.

Later, the crew knocks at our door to wake us up as we near Burgos. We have enough time to shower and eat breakfast at the bar before arriving in Burgos. The train is an hour behind when it enters the train station. Memories come to our mind when we step down onto the platform – this same train was quite delayed last year when we were tired and waiting on the platform. We are now very late to meet with our reserved taxi driver.

I called from Green Bay two days ago to confirm our arrival day and time in Burgos. Even though our conversation was in Spanish, we managed to understand each other clearly and agreed upon a meeting location in the station.

It is only a little bit after six in the morning when we reach the main hall. We see a few travelers exit the station and use the few taxis available, but there is no sign of Taxi Daniel. We wait awhile, commenting on the fact that we are an hour late, and decide to use another taxi before they all leave the station.

Sixty miles later, dozing on and off, we arrive in Santo Domingo de la Calzada. It is still dark outside and the taxi driver drops us off in the center of town, in front of the cathedral, where the trail comes through. We find our bearings and after a few backpack adjustments, we start a new year on the Camino.

*****

We have two choices of trail as we leave Santo Domingo: We can take the one which borders the main road or take the other which, in spite of a few more miles, is more peaceful, remote and nestled in nature. We opt for the quiet option after a lousy night. We stop in Granon for a break in the only café. It is packed with hikers. A lot of Spaniards, with small backpacks, are having their morning café latte. It is Saturday morning and the place is crowded, loud, and it is hard to maneuver with our backpacks.

A constant, fine drizzle has accompanied us all morning, so in spite of the noise and crowd, we have to step in and are lucky to find a small table free. The line to the bathroom is unending, so we end up staying longer than we want.

The village of Villamayor, split by the highway, is our lunch break at the restaurant Casa Leon. Fried eggs and ham, swimming in oil, is tasty but greasy for our French taste buds. We will have digesting issues later on. The owner, who takes care of us, forgot to be kind today. Short and rude, and all that in Spanish, Señor Leon is not attracting customers. I notice a St. James hiking guide on a little table, where brochures are displayed in the restaurant entrance—I should have grabbed it and made someone happy. Two days later, we meet a pilgrim who, we find out during a conversation, has forgotten his guide at the Casa Leon. Bummer! But who wants to track backward for a book?

Figure 37: Rustic Lodging, Tosantos

We reach Belorado too early in the afternoon to stop for the day. It is the town we had planned on staying for the night, so we keep going to Tosantos. The choice for lodging is minimal. The only option is the parochial albergue, which is a clean and rustic facility, three stories high, with refurbished wood floors, apparent wood beams, and to our dismay, two-inch thick, maroon mattresses, stacked up in a corner. They will be our beds for the night. We each pick one, looking for the least worn out, and find a spot for the night where we can be next to each other, with a little bit of privacy.

The large room on the third floor, meant to host a large crowd sleeping like sardines in a can, is rather empty tonight to our relief. The four parties present tonight can own a corner and spread out comfortably. The train last night, the mattress tonight—I had hoped for a better night!

Across from the house and on the other side of a little square, a family, all adults, is roasting sweet peppers in large quantities over a metal barrel, the type you often see in the ghettos. We are now in an agrarian region, where life is more simple and down to earth. Following a drink at the only cafe in town, which borders highway N120, the main road to Leon, we embark on a guided tour with other pilgrims, organized by the albergue. There is not much to do around here, once you have showered and cleaned your gear, except for visiting a little chapel nestled on the slope of a mount. We climb a small trail starting behind the village to reach a troglodyte chapel, the Virgin de la Pena, from the twelfth century. The local guide narrates its history in Spanish and asks that I translate for the English-speaking pilgrims.

We all come back to the albergue by 7 p.m. to get dinner ready. As pilgrims, we are expected to cook and set the table for sixteen people tonight in a long dining room on the first floor. After an animated dinner, a portion of pilgrims goes upstairs to a cozy room with pillows and rugs on the floor for an evening prayer, while others, including my mom and me, agree to clean and do the dishes.

The night is long, dragging, even though we go to bed at 10:30 p.m. to get up at 6:30 a.m. I wake up shortly after falling asleep, freezing in my "emergency" fleece sleeping bag. I grab the only fleece I own, the one I was using for a comfy pillow, put it on along with some socks, grab my mom's fleece that she is not using, and put it over me as a cover. Shivering all night, I doze on and off, restless. The night's temperature has seriously dropped and it is only 40 degrees when we wake up in the morning. No wonder I was cold in this old, unheated house. By the way, my mother, equipped with a normal sleeping bag, has spent a delightful night. Lesson learned—I will buy a warm, down sleeping bag for next year.

*****

If dinner was filling last night, breakfast is frugal. We hit the road at 7:40 a.m. and the sun already is shining brightly. The morning hike, about eleven miles long, is spent tramping on a variety of trails bordering pine and oak trees. The hills are huge, especially the Monte de la Pedraja, which leads to a monument at the top erected by local families, where a sign recounts in Spanish what happened here in 1936. Three hundred men were shot during the first months of the Spanish Civil War while supporting the second republic and fighting for freedom. They were murdered for their political ideal by the supporters of General Francisco Franco.

The general and dictator Franco ruled over Spain from 1939 until his death in 1975. He rose to power during the bloody Spanish Civil War when, with the help of Nazi Germany and Fascist Italy, his Nationalist forces overthrew the democratically elected Second Republic. Adopting the title of "*El Caudillo*" for The Leader, Franco persecuted political opponents, repressed the culture and language of Spain's Basque and Catalan regions, censured the media and exerted absolute control over the country. Some of these restrictions gradually eased as Franco got older, and upon his death the country transitioned to democracy.

Reaching San Juan de Ortega at noon, we are hungry, but it is too early to eat lunch. As the days go by, we figure out that it is not possible to eat lunch before one in the afternoon in Spain. Sandwiches and breakfast items are all they offer this early, which is not typical for French people who like a full meal for lunch.

The old monastery of San Juan de Ortega is a Romanesque monument commonly believed to have been built by Saint John of Ortega himself, who is buried in the church, with the help of his friend and fellow saint, Domingo de la Calzada, to serve as a resting halt for the pilgrims who walked to Santiago.

Figure 38: Poppies

The monastery has a café where pilgrims can rest and eat. We select a Serrano and cheese sandwich, in crunchy country bread and a clara, which is an acquired taste we are happy to renew since last year.

We pursue our route to Atapuerca, known in the area as a paleontological site where several limestone caves host abundant human remains discovered there in 1976. Called Sima del Elefante, "Pit of the Elephant," the site exhibits the earliest evidence of humans in Western Europe—fragments of a jawbone and teeth from 1.1 million years ago.

After a cup of tea in a café, we head out for Orbaneja Riopico, where we have planned this morning to stay at a casa rural. Orbaneja starts on a road bordered on one side by houses and on the other by corn fields. We start looking for our casa and arrive in the small center, an intersection, where stands a café. The casa rural is nowhere to be found.

Hungry, we buy a pastry at the café and run into a French fellow, which is a rare thing these days since we have been surrounded by Spaniards. We start to converse and I boldly ask him, "So, where are you sleeping tonight?"

Amused, he answers that he is going to Villafria, about three miles from here. We decide to push to the next town, too.

We are nearing Burgos, discovering the city's suburb. We follow the airport grounds for quite a while and arrive in Villafria, exhausted and eager to find a place to sleep. A small hotel, "Buenos Aires," on the main road will do. Our room in this one-star hotel seems luxurious to us after sleeping on thin mattresses on the floor last night. I take an endless shower and soak in, while my mom is unwinding on her bed. We have beaten our record today, accomplishing a twenty-four mile day hike. We are tired, sore, and a bit proud, too. Downstairs, we drink an aperitif along with olives and chips in the bar, filling up gradually with hotel guests, waiting for the dining room to open.

We meet the pilgrim we encountered in Orbaneja, who is staying here, too, and other pilgrims from different nationalities, and have dinner together. The food is less than average, but the fun company makes up for it. We step out after dinner in the dark, warm night, to pinpoint the next trail signage for tomorrow.

*****

We have four miles to arrive at the cathedral in Burgos, the one we visited last year on our way back home. A few hikers, including our dinner companions from last night, are uninterested in hiking in the suburb of a major city like Burgos. They have found out that a city bus comes by the hotel and takes you downtown in ten minutes. It is tempting, but we are stubborn and stick to our pilgrimage mode. We are determined to walk the whole trail from beginning to end, with no help, carrying our own backpacks.

The air is a little crisp this morning, only 34 degrees. We put on gloves and hats, and discover the surroundings of Burgos and the industrial zone. We're so busy looking at everything, which is a change in scenery from the peaceful countryside, we don't notice the time go by. We easily arrive in less than two hours to the old city door that leads to the cathedral.

After a few tapas and a drink in front of the majestic white cathedral, we are ready to go. The trail markers are practically nonexistent and it is tricky to get out of the city. We are forced to ask for help on three instances from locals to ensure that we are on the right path, keeping the general direction of heading west toward Santiago.

While in Tardajos for lunch, we notice a fruit and vegetable truck parked on the village square, so we buy some green grapes for the road. The only café in the village is open, but the bartender gives us such a chilly reception that we decide he does not deserve our business. Apparently pilgrims are not welcome in his facility.

In the village, we find a little convenience store, where we get a warm welcome from a friendly old lady delighted to help us gather an appetizing picnic. A nearby small, quiet square, centered by a running fountain and surrounded by empty, white stone benches, is perfect for our picnic. We take off our shoes, enjoy the shining sun, and even though the bees are irritating, we are much better off here than sitting in a busy, noisy, smelly café run by a grouchy man.

While leaving the village, a sweet grandma, sitting on a chair in the shade by her house door, calls out to us and offers fresh apples that she has just picked this morning. We gladly accept and thank her warmly. It is a precious gift before entering the mystic Meseta!

The Meseta is an arid piece of land, crossed by the Camino, which we have read and heard about for a few years now. It is finally here lying in front of us. We know it takes roughly twelve days to cross it, a distance of about 125 miles. Largely treeless and windblown, the Meseta is a high plain plateau, blistering hot in the summer and freezing cold in the winter. During the growing season, the northern Meseta shimmers golden tones with cereal crops, and then retreats to a dusty dryness. Sparsely populated, the Meseta is scattered with earth-colored villages, often camouflaged in the open plain, where only a church tower or grain silo identifies their location. Mechanization of the land has left many of the villages abandoned or inhabited only by older people, the youngest having either emigrated or moved to the large towns in search of work.

Figure 39: Nowhere to Sit; No Shade but this Little Sad Shrub

Figure 40: Mud Houses in Villages on the Meseta

Its luminous sky magnifies the distance, and this first day on the Meseta is awe-inspiring despite the hot, striking sun. We are amazed by this unfamiliar landscape and endless plateau.

Wearing our colorful hats bought last year, we cross this bare land, stark, yet majestic, dotted by little deserted villages, clean and well-kept. We arrive in Hornillos and have a drink on the main square, which has been taken over by the cackles of the pilgrims at rest, while waiting for our ride.

Yes, a ride, which is stepping out of our rule. But tonight is an exception. We have located an old mill turned into a casa rural, four miles from here, on our *Miam Miam Dodo* guide. Adventurers as we are, we take the chance. The ride is longer than we imagined, even at fast speed on narrow roads, but we eventually get there. What a delight! Entering the private property through a curvy dirt road, we are welcomed by a couple of ponies waiting for the incoming guests. After battling the hot sun and arid land, we are in a haven in the desert. We are welcomed by ducks, chickens, geese, turkeys and more as we approach the house, which is an old water-operated mill, decorated with taste, and water running under it. The yard to the side of the house is shady, and lounge chairs are laid out on the grass for guests to use. Flowers, trees and animals pop up like an oasis in the desert.

The guest house, behind the main house, is meant to host six guests in three separate rooms. These lead to a large common room with a fireplace, couches, and a long dining room table with a view of the yard.

Sunbathing in lawn chairs among nosy chickens, we rest until the air cooling down with the sunset draws us inside to sit by the fireplace. We eat dinner in the company of a couple from Spain who are celebrating the end of their adventure tonight.

We are served local specialties abundantly: zucchini soup, ham with cheese and green peppers, stuffed warm red sweet peppers, cheese and ham fried balls, Spanish blood sausage, tomato salad, pork in sauce, yogurt, and to make sure that we sleep well, our hosts get out the after-dinner liquors. We vote this our best meal of the week. This warm welcome was definitely worth stepping out of the Camino for a night via a car ride. No regrets!

*****

Tuesday morning, we board the family car for a ride back to Hornillos in the dark, where we resume our journey to Hontanas. At 3,117 feet high, the air is nippy this morning, only reaching a mere 39 degrees. Again, hats and gloves are needed. The majestic landscapes, topped with a deep blue sky, are beautiful, but it is hard to ignore the impression of walking on a highway. Pilgrims in front of us and behind us are contained on one identical path crossing the country. There is nowhere to stop, and this feeling of "keep moving or there will be a traffic jam."

A thirty-minute break in a café at Hontanas for café latte and ham sandwich, and we are off. That is, until I realize I have to backtrack to the café because I forgot my hiking stick, the same one I have carried since Le Puy en Velay, six years ago.

In the distance, we notice a man walking in the "wrong direction," or at least that is the way it feels, since we are all trying to get to the same place. A few hardcore pilgrims want to relive the real Middle Ages pilgrimage experience. As you can imagine, back then when they walked two or three months to arrive at Saint James' remains, they did not have the luxury of hopping on a plane or train to go back home. They had to do it all over again the other way.

As we get closer, this pilgrim stands out by his appearance. Accompanied by his dog, he is pushing a cart with his belongings, sort of like a hobo, but on the trail. Swearing and obnoxious, the eccentric scolds me to watch that my hiking stick doesn't intrude on his space. We later find out he has been caught in a time zone on the trail for about twenty years. A marginal soul, lost and meandering in Spain on the Camino.

Castrojeriz welcomes us with its humongous collegiate church, which we have to visit. The village is built in length on the edge of a cliff, dominated by a citadel. Well restored, the village is pleasant and we end up spending way too much time here; partly because we find a place to eat lunch, which is more of a sitting type of place. The dining room looks like a crypt, with stone walls and wine shelves all around us. We lay back a bit too much and indulge with food and wine. After this two-hour break, lazy with heavy legs, we are faced with an interminable hill that we can prepare for mentally as we see it from far away. It laces around the mountain in front of us, climbing undoubtedly to its crest. The climb, in the bright midday sun, is hard and we must take three mini-pauses before we reach the top. The summit, designed to offer rest and shade for the distressed hikers, has an awning with a sitting area. A mandatory stop to recoup!

We make it to Itera de la Vega after a long and strenuous afternoon, and are thrilled to find our hostal right away. It is located at the entrance of the village, the very first building. Pilgrims, arrived earlier, are already relaxing in the court in front of the hotel, feet up, reading and sipping cool beverages. Shortly after locating our room, which is comfortable and spacious, a clara in hand, we meet other pilgrims for a review of the day's challenges.

The village is quiet, crossed by a one-lane road. After a short visit, we find a small *mercado* and purchase food supplies for tomorrow. We have heard there might be a general strike throughout Spain, which would imply that most businesses could be closed.

We go back to our room until dinner, where we discover our first feared blisters. We take the time to care for our precious feet and pamper ourselves.

Dinner is memorable for its execrable dishes. All items are out of a can or cooked as plain as possible, matching the memory of our worst hot lunch at school. The wine, always part of the peregrino menu, makes up for it and raises our spirits; perhaps a little too much, for when we return to our bedroom, laying in the dark on our beds, an uncontrollable fit of the giggles begins over the description of the way my knees feel, moaning for deliverance at the doors of Hell. The wine is doing its magic!

*****

As the sun rises in the distance, giving a golden tone to the freshly cut wheat fields, we bid our farewells to the quiet village of Itero, where only roosters are awake and conversing with each other from one end of the village to the other. The sky, layered with high-altitude, morning clouds, announces another hot day. Our shadows, showing mostly four long and skinny legs, are walking ahead of us on the white, dusty gravel trail.

Figure 41: Walking the Meseta

The morning is uneventful, yet quite enjoyable as we cross the immense deserted Meseta. Working tractors are the only evidence of the unseen but real life of the Meseta until we reach the Canal of Castille. Attracted by the sight of water after so many miles lost in this arid desert, we feel appeased and refreshed, even though, quite ironically, all the tall trees bordering the canal are planted regretfully on the opposite bank from the path.

The canal, built from 1753 to 1849, runs for a few miles to arrive in Fromista, where a most curious set of oval locks mark the entrance of the town. The locks create a series of cascades that can overcome the greatest slope the Canal de Castilla has in any of its sections, making it a great example of hydraulic engineering. The prosperity of the region is directly linked to the building of the canal, which to this day still provides irrigation for the crops and electrical power for the local factories.

Fromista, named after the Latin word *frumentum*, depicting a fertile region, was the major producer of wheat in the Iberian region during the Roman Empire Era. The architectural richness of Fromista comes through in the Church of San Martín de Frómista, one of the finest examples of the Spanish Romanesque style.

Figure 42: Long Deserted Stretch

After a quick visit and a lengthy lunch of prosciutto and cheese sandwich, we decide to tackle the second half of this long day, a little over twenty-two miles. The twelve remaining miles are desperately timeless. The rectitude of the black-topped trail, in perfect alignment with the road, is mathematically interrupted every fifty feet by a set of two mileposts. Engraved with the blue and yellow logo, they announce to all that the Camino de Santiago is a protected path. The repetition is depressing. Blessed are we that today, due to the general strike affecting the whole country, only a few cars are on the roads. This diminishes the annoyance of this painful afternoon. Crossing a couple of sad and deserted villages, making mini-stops in the shade, my stomach is upset and the heat is not helping. Dizzy at times, we emphasize drinking and resting regularly. In the last village before Carrión de los Condes, we stop at the *albergue* and enjoy a drink.

We arrive in Carrión de los Condes in low spirits, eager to find our hostal. Located in the old center of town, our room is on the third floor, and after one last effort, we reach our haven for the night. The room is simply decorated, with tender green walls and matching green and gold curtains. I doze off for a while, while my mother showers.

Carrión de los Condes, animated as early as 7 p.m., is charming and makes up for our hard day. A town of great importance at the time of the old pilgrimages to Santiago de Compostela, its medieval origins can be seen in some of the notable buildings and in the old town. The most characteristic building of Carrión is the church of Santiago, famous for its splendid Panthocrator.

Also significant are the frieze in the church of Santa María del Camino, embellished by an Adoración de los Magos; and the convent of Santa Clara, founded in the thirteenth century, with an adjoining church and a museum, which displays sculpture and ornaments, as well as a Piedad by Gregorio Fernández.

Like two little girls, we're excited by the large option of dining places compared to our previous nights. We agree on one restaurant, which seems to offer a wide variety of specialties. Tastefully decorated with warm tones in a Spanish style, we enter the place hungry and ready for something good. It is dark outside; we waited as long as our stomachs and eyes could handle. Apparently, our idea of late is not late enough. When we sit down, to our disappointment we receive the typical peregrinos menu. After begging and a couple of explanations, we are told that the kitchen is not ready for the real menu, served after ten, for the authentic Spaniard customers.

The few occupied tables around us are indeed filled by pilgrims only, which we have encountered throughout the day. One of them, nicknamed the red sweater man, has walked as much as twenty-eight miles today and is quite happy of his accomplishment. We are first stunned and then in awe in front of so much ground covered in one day. It is something we had heard of; walking twenty-five miles and more on the Meseta, hurtling along in these wide spaces. But after our twenty-two miles today, it is barely possible to see how one can walk more.

*****

Too early for a regular breakfast in the only open café on the main square, the bread has not been delivered yet, we are lucky to find a panaderia to buy two croissants each. We have been warned about the barren next eleven miles and are ready to brave whatever will come. Loaded with snacks and water for four hours, we are on our way.

No matter how prepared you are, walking the Calzada de los Peregrinos can turn into a nightmare on this portion of the Camino. Except for a few forlorn stocky oak trees on the side of the rectilinear trail, the sun is steady and intensely present. A hat is mandatory, no matter how ridiculous we feel we look. A couple of giggles glancing at each other, and we are over it. We keep on going, consistent in our pace, even and certain, staring at the endless horizon.

Peering out in the distance to discern some signs of life, I hope . . . nothing. Nothing in sight! Finally, a little mound is forming. Calzadilla de la Cueza, a little village, the first since Carrión de los Condes. There is only one bar to welcome all the pilgrims. It is not very enjoyable, as they are a bit overloaded with orders and limited in space.

The next three and a half miles is very similar to the morning route and leads us to Ledigos, a deserted hamlet with no stores, bars or restaurants. As a last resort, we find a sidewalk in the shade, wide enough to accommodate our buttocks, with a tall, clean pinkish wall to rest our backs against. We keep an anxious eye on the pigeons sitting on the roof above our heads. The village is very rural, and the few inhabitants must be gone to work. However, we witness a comical traffic jam when a tractor backing out of his shed and a school bus returning kids home both arrive at the same time and block the intersection.

Only one and a half miles to go before we reach the hostal in Terradillos de los Templados. We arrive at two in the afternoon. The place is in the middle of nowhere, in the fields, way outside of the nearby village. Disappointed with the location and aware of the early hour, we manage to find energy to continue to the next village, one and a half miles further. One and a half miles turns into three when my mom realizes she has made an unfortunate mistake while reading the guide.

San Nicolas del Real Camino is where we will spend the night. They have one room for two left, with a toilet. The showers are upstairs. Happy to have a private room, we do not complain. The place is small and only a couple of pilgrims made the choice to stop here. We enjoy the backyard and put our swollen, bare feet in the cool, soft grass; a contrast with the dry and dusty path we treaded all day.

Our international dinner, with a German and a Canadian pilgrim, is lively, with conversation going from Spanish to German, English and French. Being polyglot can be a useful skill while on the trail!

*****

Friday, the end of the week, has come again. Our short stage allows us to leave leisurely at 8:00 a.m. this morning. Two hours on a stony trail leads us to Sahagun, known as the halfway point of the Camino Frances in Spain.

A small town located on the banks of the River Cea, Sahagún is notable for containing some of the earliest examples of the mudéjar style of architecture, a symbiosis of architectural techniques resulting from Muslim and Christian cultures living side by side. It emerged as an architectural style in the twelfth century on the Iberian Peninsula. Characterized by the use of brick as the main material, the technique did not involve the creation of new shapes or structures, unlike Gothic or Romanesque, but the reinterpretation of Western cultural styles through Islamic influences.

The taxi we called takes us to León, where our return flight leaves from. We are early enough to enjoy a visit of León, well-known for its cathedral and beautiful Parador. The Spanish *Paradores* are hotels offering luxurious accommodation in castles, palaces, convents, monasteries, fortresses and other historical buildings.

There are also a few modern Spanish hotels, built in a traditional style in areas of outstanding beauty. The Parador hotels are found throughout Spain, from Galicia in the north to Andalusia in the south.

León is the most northern province of the region Castilla y León and geographically one of the most diverse provinces in the whole of Spain with high mountains—covered in snow in winter. Steep cliffs and valleys shelter lakes and gorges on the one hand, and flat plains watered by León's many rivers and streams provide herds with pastures and farmers with land to plant cereal crops on the other. Toward the northeast, nearing the border with Galicia, the province of León is characterized by rolling countryside, round mountains covered in forests, and picturesque villages.

The Plaza Regla features a spectacular Gothic cathedral built in the twelfth century with two tall towers covered with beautiful sculptures. With wonderful, tall stained-glass windows, the cathedral is as impressive at night when it is illuminated as it is by day. The museum inside the cathedral has an interesting collection of paintings and sculptures.

The geographical diversity of the province of León is reflected in the gastronomy, too. Roasted meats, stews (notably the *cocidos maragatos)*, roasted red peppers, black sausage, potatoes, chorizos and trout are all specialties of this area of Castilla León.

The Bierzo area of León, near the border with Galicia, produces some excellent wines and liquors. Astorga is famous for its sponge cakes and *mantecadas*; Cacabelos for its cherries in orujo—similar to schnapps—and herb liquors. Cold meats and cheeses are also produced locally.

Our flight back to Paris, connecting through Barcelona, is a bit hectic. First we were delayed out of León, and then we ran into problems at check-in in Barcelona with our non-retractable, old-fashion, hiking sticks. We end up going through security with them without difficulties.

Year Seven

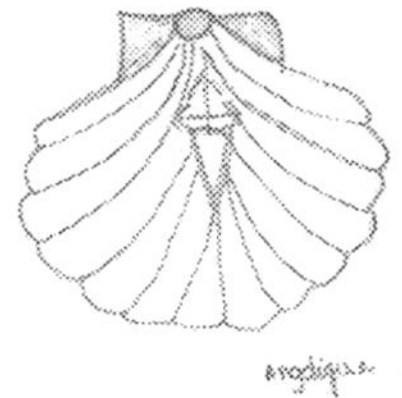

From Sahagun to Alto do Poio
140 miles in 8 days

"For we walk by faith, not by sight."
2 Corinthians 5:7

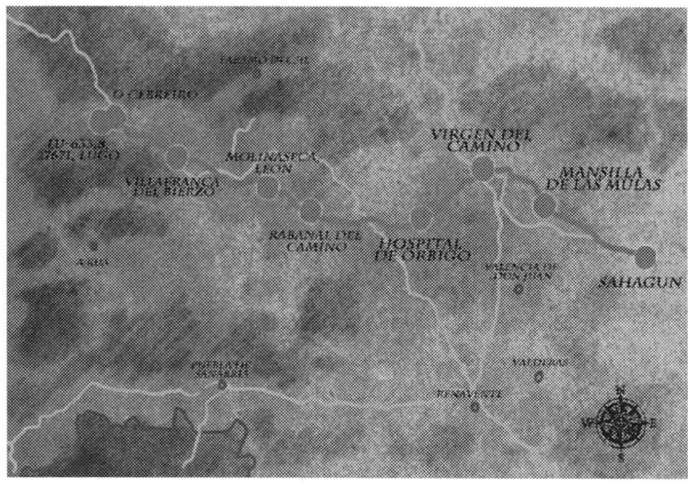

Freshly arrived from Detroit at 11:25 a.m. at Paris's Charles de Gaulle airport, I am welcomed by my parents, who are delayed due to traffic. With little time in hand, I opt for a quick run to their house, located on the west suburb of Paris, for an invigorating shower.

We have found a flight from Paris to Oviedo, on the northern coast of the Iberian Peninsula, which will bring us close to where we stopped our expedition. The flight leaves at 4:00 p.m. from De Gaulle.

The pizzeria near their house has good pizzas, Italian-style, thin and crunchy crust with all the fixings, plus a French twist. It's a great way to transition from the airplane food.

I know my backpack so well by now that it only takes me a few minutes to empty my suitcase and pack all my goodies. As a precaution, I always like to travel internationally with my backpack empty and safely protected inside a large suitcase. I have seen how luggage can get damaged—so why take a chance and arrive in Paris ready to hike and have an unusable backpack?

Our flight to Oviedo, the capital of Asturias, is smooth and on time. Catching up on family news, our stewardess jokingly teases us about our non-stop conversation during the duration of the flight.

We had reserved a taxi to drive us way inland to Sahagun, the central point of the *camino.* Upon arriving in Sahagun, our driver, a very friendly woman, gifts us with a pin of Sahagun, which we proudly hook on our backpack shoulder straps.

Our hotel, Hostal de La Codorniz, is right in town and many pilgrims are staying here. We join them in the dining room for dinner and start making connections. The meal is very local and quite tasty. My favorite tonight is the León soup made with a lot of garlic and grilled bread soaking.

*****

Friday, we wake up bright and early at 6:00 a.m. and leave in the dark at 7:15 a.m. We had planned ahead last night by walking around a bit to find the camino. We searched for any clues on sidewalks, walls or poles painted or engraved in the concrete, or perhaps an actual written sign guiding the pilgrims throughout the city to Santiago.

Each of us strikes the pose for the must-have picture, in the copper soles, holding the hiking stick of the pilgrim. It reminds everyone that here in Sahagun, the pilgrim is already halfway to the destination of Santiago.

We again have a choice of routes to pick from as we leave Sahagun. To the south is the Camino Real, nicknamed the pedestrian highway by our guide. It features stunted trees planted in an unnatural regularity, and to accommodate the flow of pilgrims, a series of rest areas designed with concrete furniture and fountains offers a monotonous, almost depressing option to cross the meseta. To the north is the Calzada Romana, definitely a more adventurous route that we hear is used more by foreigners than Spaniards. This trail, very straight as well, is wild and not tamed by man.

We opt for the quieter and wilder path, since we read the trail is well-marked, so why not? We follow our instincts at an unmarked crossroad and pick one which leads us, after a few confusing turns, in the wrong direction. So here we are on this first day, hiking off-piste, aiming for the general direction we want to go to. After crossing a large high-speed train track, very carefully and not without hesitation, knowing how fast European trains travel, we merge back with the trail, happy to find it again despite the extra thirty minutes of hiking.

Three hours later, Calzadilla de los Hermanillos, the only possible stop along the way, appears like a mirage in the desert. The hostal is like paradise! We are given a hearty welcome by the thoughtful owner; who understands what pilgrims desire when they reach his place. He has arranged a well-decorated garden with abundant vegetation, where umbrellas offer shade over cozy lawn chairs and tables. We order our first ham and cheese sandwich, and for the cherry on top, the owner kindly brings us a homemade, delicious, seafood paté on toast. Other pilgrims arrive and, like us, remove their hiking boots to inspect their feet and look for any damage. The feet heat up much quicker here and the potential for blisters is greater.

Later in the afternoon, after a sad five-minute stop sitting on pit gravel along the edge of the trail, we run out of water. We are quite parched when we reach Reliegos. My feet are hurting; blisters have pierced through my skin, inconveniently on my toes, which require attention. Originally our stop for the night, the village has only one form of lodging, an *albergue*. Lately, we have heard through *radio chemin* about bed flea issues and are a little leery about sleeping in an albergue.

It is only four o'clock, and according to our guide, the next town is in four miles, a little more than an hour and a half. We are still mentally fresh and feel strong and cocky, so we decide to go to Mansilla, which has two or three hostals.

We are exhausted upon arrival. My knees are achy and we settle for the Hostal del Puente, whose manager welcomes us like a prison officer who forgot to be amiable. Our room is on the third floor. Our backpacks are unbearable by now, and my knees don't want to climb the flight of stairs. Worn out by twenty-four miles of hiking and leftover jetlag, I reach our room, shower and take a little siesta. What a start for a first day!

Dinner is at 8:30 p.m.; the choice is minimal but turns out to be tasty. We dine next to two tables of French hikers, a rare thing these days, being so far away from France.

*****

Today, we are planning on hiking a bit less than yesterday, so we set our alarm clock for 6:45 a.m. and leave at 8:15 a.m.; enough time to bandage our feet and care for our blisters. The mood down in the cafeteria this morning is as iffy as last night for breakfast. The waitress serves us breakfast with little enthusiasm, and it is difficult to obtain what we need.

The morning trail is pleasant, traveling through verdant and lush agricultural landscapes, walking mainly on a quiet little road. After more than two hours, we pause for a *tortilla de patatas*; in Spain, the dish goes by two names: tortilla de patatas or *tortilla española*. The English translation, potato omelet, is not the best fit, since a Spanish tortilla is more about potatoes than eggs, and the word omelet doesn't really conjure up the right image. Whether served warm, cool, or at room temperature, it makes an excellent breakfast, lunch, dinner or snack. It is available in most cafés bright and early in the morning, and gives us all the energy we need to hike for two more hours to reach León, the capital.

Tortilla de Patatas

Serves: 4

Ingredients:

- 1/2 pint of olive oil
- 5 medium baking potatoes, peeled, sliced and lightly sprinkled with salt
- 1/2 yellow onion, chopped
- 3 garlic cloves, minced
- 6 eggs
- Salt and pepper

Method:

Heat the olive oil in a skillet and add the potato slices. Try to keep the potato slices separated so they will not stick to each other.

Cook over medium heat turning occasionally. Add the onions and garlic and cook until the potatoes are tender.

Drain leaving about 3 tablespoons of oil in the skillet.

Meanwhile, whisk the eggs, salt and pepper. Combine the potatoes, and stir to coat with the egg.

Add the egg-coated potatoes to the hot oil in the skillet, spreading them evenly to completely cover the base of the skillet.

Lower the heat to medium and continue to cook, shaking the pan frequently.

Using a plate to cover the skillet, flip the omelet. Add 1 tablespoon oil to the pan and slide the omelet back into the skillet on its uncooked side.

Cook until completely set.

Allow the omelet to cool, and cut it into wedges.

Serve warm or at room temperature with a side of greens.

As we near León, the scenery changes from fields to industrial buildings, following highways and bypasses. However, at all times we are protected from the roads, never too close, with only the city noise to remind us that we are now in a large conurbation.

It is with great pleasure that we meet again with León, a beautiful city rich with many monuments, including a beautiful, gothic cathedral built in the thirteenth century, and a Parador. As a blink to last year's halt in León, we return to the same café on the Plaza de la Regla, facing the cathedral, for a drink.

We take the opportunity of being in a major city to look for a fine restaurant to enjoy some of the local specialties. It can be difficult to find locations that offer fine dishes in small villages. Surrounded by well-dressed couples visiting for the weekend, our appearance as hikers makes a few eyebrows rise, but our good manners and big smiles make up for it. Our lunch is excellent, rich and filling. We indulge in an appetizer and a main course while trying not to think about what will happen when we have to load our backpacks and hit the road. We are focused on enjoying the moment. The piquillos a la maresco, our appetizer, are divine.

Piquillo peppers come from the Navarra region of northern Spain. Named for their distinctive beak-like shape, these bright red peppers are handpicked in the fall, fire-roasted, and peeled. Some are even roasted right in the field after being harvested. Traditionally, piquillos are stuffed with either seafood or meat, but their uses extend far beyond.

With heavy bellies, we courageously resume our pilgrimage, saying goodbye to a luxurious lifestyle for a while. We have only two hours of walking in the suburb of León to reach our evening town, Virgen del Camino.

Legend states that the Virgin appeared in front of Alvar Simon, a shepherd, on July 2, 1505, and asked him to build a shrine. As he was asking for a sign, she sent with her slingshot a stone six hundred feet away, which one turned into a large rock. In 1513, a chapel was erected in that site. Miracles multiplied at the site, arousing pilgrimages which still take place today on September 15 and 29, and October 5. The chapel has been replaced by a church, inaugurated in 1961 and designed by Francisco Coello, a Portuguese Dominican monk architect, in a startling contemporary style. The sculptor José María Subirachs erected thirteen statues, in a clear Modernist style, of the twelve Apostles standing above the west door, with Saint James looking toward Santiago.

Our hostal stands just across from the church, facing with respect this awe-inspiring edifice. After a short investigation, we find that no breakfast is served, and tomorrow being Sunday morning, the neighboring bars do not open until nine, much too late of a start for us pilgrims. We'll have to stop at the grocery store a few streets away.

Ambling in the meandering streets, we come across a lively section with outdoor restaurants. The ambiance is typically southern, where people mostly live outside, and kids, on their bikes or playing with their trucks, play in the street while the parents socialize, having tapas and aperitif with their neighbors.

We set our minds on a seafood restaurant, where our host sits us at a table outside, right on the narrow sidewalk bordering a lively one-way street the size of a wide alley. The appetizer we both selected comes in a medium-size tureen, which releases an appetizing aroma of crab soup. One bowl, followed by another, leads to the arrival of our main course, as aromatic as the previous course. A plate, designed with style, comes filled with calamari cuisined with a black ink sauce. Even though eating a black-colored dish can be surprising, it's very tasty!

Walking back to our hostal, we are amazed to think that, on this small square facing the church, no less than 50,000 people are expected to arrive in two days. The dynamic of this small town will be turned upside down.

We notice that we have encountered friendlier people since entering the city and its suburb, in comparison to the preceding farming areas on the meseta. The harsh conditions in which those people have to live must embitter their personality.

Back to the room, we must allot time for the care of our obvious toe blisters, swollen and filled with a clear warm liquid, shouting for pity.

*****

Our enthusiasm is feeble as we start the day with a frugal breakfast in the hostal room and have in mind the layout of the day, especially when reading the narratives of previous hikers depicting the expanse of land as long, deserted, plain, and endless. The *Paramo*!

With a mean altitude of 2,625 feet above sea level, the Paramo is listed as an old desert that can be visualized as a sort of platform between two rivers. Two routes are proposed to reach Hospital de Orbigo on the other side of the so-called desert.

The Camino Real is the shortest alternative. Almost twenty-five miles long, this authentic, historical path is noted in many publications. Nowadays it is coated with blacktop and serves as a main highway to Santiago. The Calzada de los Peregrinos is the more scenic route, far from major roads. Dirt roads and serene, small roads alternate easily thanks to a well-marked signalization.

After studying our options for a bit, it becomes obvious that the Calzada de los Peregrinos, the longer option, is where we belong, away from the tumult of the traffic brought by highway 120.

Our salvation, is now visible ahead of us. From early on this morning, we have been able to discern the contour of the chain of mountains that will save us from this interminable plateau called Meseta. We reach the small town of Chozas de Abajo at an opportune time for a respite with refreshments at the village bar. We quickly jabber with pilgrims from Canada and Washington, D.C.

The rest of the morning is mind-numbing, with nothing new to look at, nothing stunning to be awestruck; just the same old, long, infinite, plain landscape. Not much is said verbally, but the backpack takes over the conversation. It quietly, but forcefully, reminds me with each step of the burdensome weight of what I considered back home to be the bare minimum to bring along. The mind, in idle mode while not absorbed by its surroundings, looks for another subject to discuss. This morning, the subject often revolves around a sensation of agony, oscillating from a mix of backache to throbbing pain in the shoulders, and burning or stinging within the toes.

Figure 43: Taking the Cows to the Barn by Bike

"Are we almost there?" I start hearing a little pleading voice behind me. "When are we stopping for lunch? I need a break," my mom says in a desperate voice.

The small village of Villar de Mazarife welcomes pilgrims with a medieval-style mosaic at the entrance. It depicts a group of ten pilgrims dressed in the style of the old days with long coats and tall staff, standing on each side of the Mudéjar-style parish Iglesia de Santiago, which has several images of the Saint inside and many stork nests on the roof. We do not stop in Villar de Mazarife, but shortly afterward we do.

It is around half past noon when we finally find an accessible field, just harvested, where a few white beans that did not make it into the truck are still laying there.

We improvise and eat what we can find in our backpacks, which is not much but sufficient—prunes and cheese. The priority is on resting in the sun, lying on a cobbled-up lawn chair—one could say with a lot of imagination, and appreciative of little after much effort—made with a sarong and a backpack for the head rest. We easily ignore the usual bumps from the dirt mounds on the uneven ground that would drive anyone insane on a regular day.

In Villavente, our next stop, we pause at the bar to eat an omelet and engage in conversation with the only other patron, a French fellow from Boulogne in the Parisian suburb, who is enjoying a glass of white wine and another and another. It is three in the afternoon. Looking rather tipsy and excited to meet French pilgrim ladies, he sits by us and tells us his story, and how back in Paris he has been going to the association welcoming the St. James pilgrims every Friday night. He kindly writes the address on a piece of paper for us to meet him there in later days.

Continuing our route to Hospital, we meet again with the Camino Real just when we are about to arrive in town. If my mom spent extra time in the bathroom this morning reflecting on the effects of the delicious crab soup from last night, it is only upon reaching Hospital that my stomach expresses its discontent by means of unbearable cramps. Bent in half, entirely forgetting about my heavy backpack, I moan all the way to the entrance of the village.

Figure 44: 13th Century Bridge, 20 Arches in Hospital de Orbigo

It is late afternoon when we arrive in front of the most popular bridge all the way along the Camino. A pilgrim's hospital that existed here in the Middle Ages gives the town its name; however, there has been a settlement here on the banks of the Órbigo River since the Roman times. The town has witnessed many battles in its long history as a strategic point on the Roman route connecting the Roman city of Astorga and the silver mines of the Bierzo region with France.

However, it was not any of these military engagements that made the town's name famous for all time, but rather a contest of a more romantic nature that took place in the mid-fifteenth century. Don Suero was in love with a lady by the name of Doña Leonor de Tobar, who unfortunately did not feel the same way. This knight, considering himself a prisoner of her love, decided to wear an iron collar around his neck every Thursday as a symbol of being enslaved by his love for her.

As a way to impress both the lady he loved and King Juan II, along with freeing himself from his enslavement, Don Suero decided to embark on a surprising joust in the old knight style. At a meeting in January 1434, Suero proposed to the King that he would break three hundred lances on the bridge over the río Órbigo, close to a pilgrim hospital run by the order of San Juan, Saint John, and only when he had accomplished this would he remove his iron collar.

Many knights arrived from all places encompassing Germany, Italy, Portugal, and especially from the kingdom of Aragón. The tournament started on July 10, 1434, and lasted a month. Don Suero and his nine fellow knights defeated sixty-eight men, killing only one, and managed to break nearly two hundred lances. The men who were judging the contest decided that was enough, and during a ceremony removed the iron collar from Suero's neck.

This thirteenth-century bridge, the longest one on the Camino at approximately 670 feet, has twenty arches. The river, the Río Órbigo flows through only three arches and doesn't seem to warrant such a lengthy bridge, but prior to the building of a dam at Barrios de Luna, the river was a lot wider.

Reserved for pedestrians, the bridge itself is one of the best examples of a Roman structure in the whole of Spain. It has been rebuilt on several occasions following damage inflicted by floods that collapsed some of its arches. It also suffered damage in the nineteenth century when two of its arches were blown up at the hands of the retreating English army, allied with Spain, as they fled Napoleon's army. Fortunately for contemporary pilgrims, restorations have preserved its medieval appearance. The bridge we see today looks just as it would have to the eyes of the noble revelers gathered on the banks of the Órbigo River for the legendary Suero de Quiñones jousts.

On the bridge at Hospital de Orbigo, a plaque commemorating the tournament shows the names of the ten knights who were involved. The plaque also contains a text roughly translated as such:

To be rescued from the prison in which his lady held him

And desiring long lasting fame

He set out with nine other knights

To defend the honorable pass close to this bridge

Breaking lances with more than 70 knights

That to the pilgrim road of the Apostle St James

They came from Castilla, Aragon and Cataluña

From Valencia, Portugal and Britain

From Italy and Germany

The Fiesta de las Justas del Paso Honroso takes place in a field close to the bridge in commemoration of the legend in early June every year since 1997. The story is mentioned in Don Quijote and may have been an inspiration for the old knight himself.

Weary and unable to fully appreciate this famous landmark, we rush to the first hotel we stumble upon, which happens to have an unrivalled location. Our small bedroom opens up over an outdoor terrace overlooking the drawn-out bridge, which is as long as some hamlets we have crossed these past days. Relieved, showered and pampered, we treat ourselves to a clara with olives and chips on the terrace below. We are entertained by the regular arrival of pilgrims, watching their faces and styles, including the noteworthy man who catches my eye clothed with a Scottish kilt; but as we find out later, originating from Germany.

If the location is outstanding, the food is less than passable and indisputably overpriced, to our great surprise the next morning when we pay our bill after breakfast.

*****

The mountain chain to the west is more visible today, announcing a radical change in terrain and culture, the Galician region. The topography chart, outlining the gradients of today's itinerary, confirms the slight but constant ascension we are about to walk. It is a pleasing thought, however, after spending 125 miles on the flat Meseta.

Heading out as soon as the sun is up at almost 7:45 a.m., we have a superb view on the mounts of León. There is a choice of routes available again today, and we elect the more natural pathway away from the busy highway 120, which is bordered by the historical Camino Real. The chosen itinerary crosses many villages on a main road called Calle Real, persuading the hesitant pilgrim of the authenticity of this route. Four hours is needed to reach Astorga, during which the land undulates, the path navigates curves, climbing and descending amongst cultivated fields and green oak woods. The metamorphosis is evident and so pleasing to the soul, never a feeling of monotony. We finally reconnect with what we know to be a hiking trail, where every bend brings some suspense as to what will be on the other side. It is a mind game that makes hiking fun. The path is a bit crowded this morning, but nevertheless agreeable.

Both paths meet at the Cross Santo Toribio, from where we have a great view of Astorga. The town is a tiny place with a big personality. As a settlement, it dates back to Celtic times and is a stopping place on the Camino de Santiago. However, this is not just a place for religious spirituality, it is also a mecca for any serious chocoholic. It happens to be the place where chocolate was first introduced to Europe. The town takes both things seriously. There is one museum dedicated to the Camino and another to chocolate. Strewn with historical landmarks as a testimonial of its intense past, the town welcomes backpackers as well as globetrotters, giving us the feeling of being on vacation.

Astorga is the capital of the county of Maragatería in the province of León. It offers a rich, medieval legacy, the result of its location at the crossroads of two major pilgrim roads to Santiago de Compostela and the Ruta de la Plata—Silver Road. Its walled town preserves churches, convents and hospitals, taking travelers back to the purest tradition of the Pilgrim's Road. The *Puerta del Sol* leads into the fortified area, where the cathedral is the outstanding feature. Construction on the current building began in the fifteenth century, although work continued until the seventeenth century. As a result, its layout preserves Gothic, Renaissance and Baroque elements, featuring works by masters from all the periods.

Astorga has the privilege of housing a work by Antonio Gaudi, the most important modernist architect in Spain and one of the most famous in the world. When the old Archbishop's Palace was destroyed by fire in 1886, the bishop of the town of chocolate commissioned Gaudi to build a new Episcopal edifice. The construction of the palace began in 1887 and was not completed until 1893. The palace has the aspect of a castle, mansion and temple with its impressive exterior constructed with white granite. Constructed in a neo-gothic style, it presents a series of elements with apparent military function such as battlements, towers and others as viewpoints and terraces. Gaudí's creative genius—and the curves, shapes, and ornamentations it produced—literally changed the face of architecture and building technology during the late nineteenth and early twentieth centuries. Gaudí recognized the formal order proper to most architecture before his time, and deliberately turned it upside down. As a result, his buildings seem strikingly unique and almost surreal even a century later.

We sat at a café right across from the palace and the cathedral for a bite of a tortilla frances and tortilla de patatas. Only a short pause is permitted, since we still have to walk fourteen miles this afternoon to reach Rabanal del Camino.

Fortunately, we will progress to Rabanal on a slow slope all the way there, which eases our task. To motivate ourselves while looking at the map, we decide to stop for a mini-halt, no more than fifteen minutes, at each little village we run into on the way there. They are three little dots on the map, evenly spaced out. Perfect!

The afternoon does not resemble anything we saw this morning. The straight lines are back, with little shadow to offer, and a lot of asphalt. It is perfect for all the bikers that pass us, alone or in little groups, appearing and disappearing in the horizon. We are alerted by the sound of their conversation and look at them a bit envious of their rolling machine, carrying their backpack.

It is 90 degrees in the shade, a bit much for a low-shade hiking trail. Our feet have expanded, trapped in their confined area, and it seems as though we are walking in rubber boots after the water ran over the top. A flick flock impression!

A man provides some entertainment with a surprising show for us and all the ladies that walk by. We glance at him as he squats in a field to our right, not sure what he is up to, and to our great surprise, he unveils his precious parts right there in the field. Who would expect an exhibitionist, right here in the midst of nature, miles and miles away from a city? I recall seeing one in Paris years back, on the opposite platform, while waiting for the metro. He had walked toward me with his long trench coat, and with a quick gesture had exposed his nakedness to my eyes.

But here, on the Camino, who would have thought!

Listening to radio camino—the nickname hikers made up to describe the word of mouth used by all to communicate on minor or major facts worth mentioning—we find out in the following villages that many girls and ladies have seen him today. It provides great fuel for animated conversations.

Approaching Rabanal, we make one last stop at a 100-year-old oak tree known as the tree of the pilgrims, where we meet a devoted man and his twelve-year-old son, both pilgrims, off their bikes and cleaning the area of littering items.

Halfway down the main street upon entering the village, a little old lady, seated on the step of her house, summons us to come by her. Obedient and intrigued, we approach her. At her feet is a basket full of rustic, deformed tomatoes. Eager to share her daily harvest, she hands us a handful of tomatoes to help us out on our route. So sweet!

Rabanal, which ten years ago looked like a ghost town, is alive again thanks to the camino. A group of Englishmen from the Confraternity of St. James settled here and renovated the whole village. They opened two restaurants and two lodging options, and turned the ghost town into a lively community. The village, built in length, has a typical mountain look with houses made of irregularly stacked stones. The English inn is very British, and after a tour of the village, it is a perfect spot for a drink in a cozy environment.

Dinner takes place back at the hotel we are staying at, El Refugio, in a crowded dining hall broken up into different areas. As guests of the hotel, our table has been reserved. We are seated near other guests in an elevated smaller section, apart from the main room.

Our room, number 21, is the best so far this year. Opening over the main strip, we have an encompassing view over the whole village, showing its restored houses with arched entrances made of massive stones from the neighboring fields.

*****

Breakfast is amazing. What a change! After eating Spanish croissants for a few days, large and sweetened with a sticky sugary coating, it is a delight this morning to see on our breakfast table thick, long slices of country bread, grilled. A great start for the day.

Our late start at 8:20 a.m. is partly due to the later sunrise as we inch our way to the west. Leaving Rabanal at 3,972 feet of altitude, we keep climbing to 4,724 feet on a swerving little blacktopped road for two and a half miles until we reach Foncebadon. It is a village in ruins, where a dirt road leads to the one and only alive place, a hostal being restored. The woman in charge has rooms for pilgrims, a mini store with convenience items, and a bar to refresh all the pilgrims who just ascended the last nine hundred feet. Large wooden tables and tree stumps for seats are placed across the streets for pilgrims to rest and eat a bite. We do just that, in company of the house dog, a sizeable, very friendly light brown female in need of petting time.

The moorland is becoming more and more bleak as we reach higher altitudes. The camino ascends patiently to the pass of the Cruz de Ferro at 4,900 feet, one of the highest points on the camino. A small, metal cross, erected at the end of a sixteen-foot pole, stands proudly at the top and represents Christianity in its greatness. It can be seen from far away and served as a guiding point to pilgrims back in the days when heavy snowfalls would cover the signage. Planted in a cairn, the cross is a known stop among modern pilgrims who traditionally bring their own rock, carried all along the way from home, to add to the cairn. It's a gesture also known by mountain people as a guiding tool for others. As we stand in line for a souvenir picture, where everyone offers to take a picture of the party ahead of them, we enjoy the sight which opens up on almost barren mountains.

Manjarin, another abandoned village, reminds us of the old times when people lived in these remote areas, tending to their flocks of sheep. Tomas, an original figure who is famous on the trail, has established a hostal on the fringe of the ruined village. Bright colors and quantities of artifacts, among which stands a Templar Cross, are eye-catching from far back and make this a must-stop.

Figure 45: Tomas' Hostal in Manjarin

We pursue our ascension to yet a higher pass, known as the highest one, and before descending toward Acebo, we spot a large slate, perfect for a temporary bench, where we can enjoy the plump tomatoes of the obliging grandma from Rabanal.

Acebo is a charming old village, the first village in the Bierzo. It is noticeably different in its construction, with slate roofs replacing tile roofs, and one can see outside stairs and covered pathways. The village is built along the one street, in perfect shape and offers a few options for eating.

We find the ideal restaurant for our lunch pause. We are led through the dining room to an outdoor patio, where we step into a garden with tables set in the grass. Flowers and abundant lush vegetation brings a sense of coolness. This is also a casa rural where pilgrims' laundry is hanging in one section of the yard, chairs are waiting for tired hikers, and a handful of cats are welcoming everyone.

How good it feels to remove our shoes and socks, and lay our feet on cool, soft grass while we eat. Determined to sample a local dish, we order a trout prepared with ham a la plancha with a salad. The food is great. What a treat after all the sandwiches and tortillas we have been eating.

The cats are attracted by the scent of fish. They act starved and keep begging for scraps. We are outside and it is easy to feed them bits and pieces. No other customers are eating, so the cats have their full attention on our table. What happens next is one of these things you had to be there to laugh! As you might know, in Europe, many times when you order fish, it is served dressed on your plate, so there is some tedious work of making filets before you eat. After cleaning my trout, I proceed to hand out the fish skin to one of the cats sitting on the grass on the other side of the table, next to my mother. As I motion to throw the sticky, slimy fish skin across the table, it unexpectedly sticks to my fingers a bit too long and affects its trajectory. It lands on my mother's left cheek as she is eating. Stunned and not knowing what hit her, she looks at me shocked. After a moment, I see her eyes change from shocked to disgust as she understands what hit her, and I start an uncontrollable laugh, not so funny to her.

Figure 46: This Trout was Tasty! The Skin was Sticky, I Heard!

After an hour, we resume our descent to the next village named Riego de Ambros. There is a noticeable change in vegetation as we descend into the valley of Bierzo. Walnut and chestnut trees are replacing the green-leaf oaks, moss is covering tree trunks and stones, and in the distance to the west, a mountain chain stands as the last obstacle before Galicia. Down a narrow pebbly path, we make our way down and arrive in an hour's time to Riego. There, at the bottom of the trail, is a road. Across from it sits a large, fenced-in property where a long grass field separates the house from the road. A table and a few bright red chairs are set near the fence, under a large tree and a few steps away from the wide-open gate. We accept the informal invitation and sit for a while.

We follow a constantly descending path to reach the village of Molinaseca, which is at an altitude of only 1,900 feet. This is a bit hard on the knees and we are glad to arrive. We use the medieval bridge to enter Molinaseca and start our search for a place to sleep. To our disappointment, the first hostal is full. We continue our research and find out that many hotels and hostals are full. We are becoming uneasy with the thought of finding something. Luckily, a fancy hotel sends us to an address in the back streets. We are to ask for a room at the little grocery store, not bigger than a single room. We are welcomed by an older woman, sitting on a chair right outside the store, who speaks a little bit of French and is overjoyed to communicate with us. Her daughter, working inside, steps out and confirms that she has a room for us across the street in an apartment building. No breakfast or dinner is possible, but there are plenty of options in town. We are to wait here a while in her mom's company while she goes to prepare the room.

With groceries for the next day covered, we sip a drink by the river and write our notes for the day. Later, we find an unpretentious restaurant for supper and have a good night's sleep.

*****

We leave the apartment building at 7:30 am after eating breakfast in the room. It is pitch black outside, but we are in the village for a mile or so and we can see where we are going. We follow a lit-up road with sidewalks, and toward the end of the village we stumble over a hardcore albergue. The beds are set outside on a terrace surrounding the building, protected only by an awning. It is one step up from camping.

We are about to cross the whole length of the Bierzo Valley, which is completely surrounded by mountains. Vineyards and intensive crops punctuate our pathway, keeping us away again from the historical tracing, spoiled by traffic and blacktop. The vineyards, benefiting from abundant water and hot sun, yield a good wine called the berciano. Red or whites alike are superb.

A third of the way into our day, we arrive in Ponferrada, the last major town along the French route of the Way of Saint James before it reaches its destination of Santiago de Compostela. The first records of Ponferrada are as a former citadel in Roman times. From the eleventh century, the rise in pilgrimages to Santiago de Compostela spurred the appearance of the hamlet of Pons Ferrata, located on the Pilgrim's Route to Santiago de Compostela. It is named in this way because of the building on a bridge reinforced with iron. In 1178, King Fernando II of León placed this flourishing settlement under the custody of the Order of the Temple.

The Knights Templar used the site of a primitive Roman fortress to build a castle in which they settled, and at the same time, protected the passing pilgrims. This favored demographic growth and led to the commercial development of the area.

After enjoying a ColaCao and a croissant on a terrace on Plaza del Ayuntamiento, facing the town hall, we head out toward VillaFranca. We pass by Camponaraya at lunchtime, but we're unable to find an appealing restaurant in this working town. We eventually sit at a Heineken-green table on a small square, near the main road. We order a Cannelloni dish out of a picture-type of menu. It is frozen and so nasty that we are unable to finish it, even though we're starved.

Needing a mental boost, we are glad to find the Bierzo wine co-op where ladies, hikers like us, are sitting outside around large wine barrels serving as tables, drinking and eating. We step inside and order wine to taste, served with a *pincho* for a mere Euro. Our spirits are up as we savor the local wine outside and observe the variety of vehicles reflecting small- or large-run operations, packed with freshly cut grapes being brought in for weighing.

The afternoon is punctuated with stops and encounters, including one with a group of six French hikers from Caen in Normandy, with whom we climb a trail for about two and a half miles.

We later reach VillaFranca with sore feet. Despite a few hitches in finding the village square where our lodging is located, climbing stairs, and descending others, we rejoice at the sight of our hotel. It is a real hotel tonight, the only one this week, and we appreciate the treat. Located on the main square of the village, the hotel is newly renovated in modern style. We feel spoiled for a few seconds before hastening in indulgence.

The last significant town before Santiago, Villafranca del Bierzo is believed to have been founded by French monks of the Cluny order. They built a monastery here called el Monasterio de Santa Maria de Cluniaco during the years following the discovery of Santiago's body in 813 in order to service the needs of the many pilgrims who passed this way. As the monks were French, the village became known as Villafranca, or town of the French.

Figure 47: Local Specialties in VillaFranca del Bierzo - Sausages and a Knuckle of Ham

Just as you enter the town, you come across the twelfth century Iglesia de Santiago. This church was granted the privilege of providing absolution to the pilgrims who were too ill to continue along the Camino to Santiago. This absolution was received at the Puerta del Perdón, the door of forgiveness that can be found at the side of the church. In terms of pilgrim architecture, the town once had as many as eight monasteries and six pilgrim hospitals.

A short visit and we rush for a drink and dinner to follow. We're famished and start with spicy mussels. Feeling brave and rather daring, we blindly order a local dish. The service is excellent, the warm night is delightful and the food is to die for. The main course is a great sample of two local specialties; the *botillos*, savory large sausages, and *lacon con grelos*, a knuckle of ham prepared with turnip greens. Stuffed, we are obliged to go for a digestive walk after dinner. We had our revenge over our nasty lunch.

*****

Looking ahead, the topography is crystal clear: seventeen miles, all in ascension, going from 2,000 feet to 4,300 feet, to end at the emblematic mountainous and minuscule village of O'Cebreiro, the entering door of Galicia.

With this in mind, we have breakfast at the café downstairs and leave early, in the dark, from the sleepy square. This morning we are trapped, hiking in a corridor between the road and the river, following the curves of the mountain. The glacial wind rushes into the corridor, and our thin gloves, fleece hood and paper-thin scarf make an inadequate shield. We are cold and moving fast. Our first stop is in Pereje, a village with a medieval atmosphere, where we warm up with a hot drink. Other hikers are sitting here as well. A family of three catches our eye, all carrying their backpacks, mom, dad and their furry animal. The sturdy little dog has his own backpack, cleverly conceived with a couple of pouches on each sides. Resting on his back, he is drinking out of a fabric bowl that once done, fits conveniently back in one pouch.

We continue our ascension, still canalled in a corridor between the river, which is now far down in its bed, and mountains, catching glimpses of a highway crossing over valleys on sky-high viaducts. In Trabadelo, we stop for a tortilla de patatas at the albergue, served with good country-style bread. We are surrounded by mountains and forests. The change from earlier in the week, when we walked the last miles of the Meseta, is so satisfying.

Later on, we reach Vega de Valcarce, a mile-long stretched out village of little interest except for its sizeable sawmill. The group of French hikers we met yesterday is sitting at a café and we join them for lunch.

They quickly share their misadventure from the night before in Villafranca. They had planned to sleep at the municipal albergue in dormitories, when upon their arrival, they found out that the albergue had to close down one of the dormitories on account of the discovery of bedbugs. Reddish-brown in color and about a quarter-inch long and three-quarters of an inch wide, are notorious hitchhikers, and pilgrims are ideal unwitting vehicles that spread infestation along the camino. Even though albergues are increasingly being fumigated for insects, it is a good idea to ask to see a certification of recent fumigation when rumors of bedbugs are circulating. We all reflect on the basics of staying free of bedbugs, which consists of feeling along the seams of the mattress, as this is where the insects often hide during the day. Other signs of bugs, they tell us, include blood stains or tiny black spots, like poppy seeds or pen marks, which are bedbug excrement.

In case you ever get too close to these repulsive creatures, such as a bite, there is a basic protocol to follow. Assume that your belongings are carrying bugs and/or eggs. There are several ways to rid your belongings of bedbugs. Set out all your belongings on the grass and spray with a bug repellent that is effective for bed bugs. Let your items dry in the sun, then wash them in a washing machine with hot water and dry in a hot dryer. If you are in a larger city, you can take all your clothes, sleeping bag and pack to be dry cleaned. For fabric items that cannot be machine washed, spray with bug repellent and place in a ziplock bag or another airtight bag for 24 hours, then hand wash in hot water. Yuck! Glad we stayed in a hotel last night. Spoiled, but glad!

Quiet hamlets intersperse our early afternoon as we start the stiff climb toward La Faba, at first on a sun-bathed blacktop road which eventually turns into a shady, old, stony path. Worn out, we reach La Faba where our companions are already resting in the shade, sitting on a few chairs along a low stone wall across from a small bar. They used the road to climb instead of the path and arrived ahead of us.

Figure 48: O'Cebeiro, Medieval Village

We have only two and a half miles left before reaching O'Cebreiro, about one hour and ten minutes, in a constant climb, immersed in a splendid environment, high mountainous landscapes, with purple heath everywhere. It is hot and the heat is distressing as we climb with no shade. Here and there we find a little shade and enjoy a couple of minutes rest until we enter O'Cebreiro. Before arriving in the village, we pass the welcome border marker to the Galician province. Even though the Galician culture has spread out of its frontier, as we noticed these last couple of days, we are now officially in Galicia, the last province before the Atlantic Ocean.

Galicia is unlike anywhere else in Spain and is best described as similar to Ireland, Brittany or Cornwall. The coastline is comprised of tiny coves, beautiful sandy beaches, flanked by high cliffs, fishing ports and sheltered harbors. Inland, the region is green and wooded, especially along the valleys where trees overlook lush meadows and orchards. Known as the land of a thousand rivers, Galicia is separated from the rest of the country by extensive mountain ranges on all sides and only the river Miño separates it from Portugal.

More than eighty percent of the people speak Galician well, though nearly all of them also speak Castellano, the official Spanish, and may even choose to use it most of the time. Galician is known as Galego in the local language.

Galicia is a mythical place and has a great tradition of folk stories and legends. Galicians like to think of themselves as having deep Celtic roots and affinities with Ireland. In fact, one local myth is that Galicia was "colonized" by settlers from Ireland and Scotland in the third century BC. This, of course, would make the Galicians very different from the rest of Spain. As for superstitions—legends of werewolves and witches, goblins and fairies continue to feature in the lives of many. Most visibly, fortune telling is a widespread activity in Galicia. Whether Celtic or not, the Galicians certainly do uphold one Spanish tradition – they throw fiestas whenever they can.

Entering the old town, there is a definite Celtic atmosphere. The remote hamlet of O Cebreiro is perched on a high ridge and welcomes visitors to Galicia. With extensive views across the verdant but harsh Galician landscape, O Cebreiro brings us back to the past with its pallozas, round stone huts with straw roofs the villagers used to live in until as recently as the 1960s.

A must in O Cebreiro is a visit to the pre-Romanesque church, the oldest remaining fully intact on the Pilgrim's Route to Santiago de Compostela. It contains a Holy Grail that some consider to be sacred and others miraculous. Founded in the year 836, Santa María la Real rings its bells during the winter to guide the pilgrims through the mists. It proudly houses relics from a Eucharistic miracle that occurred in the town in the fourteenth century in which a priest celebrated Mass without truly believing his actions—in fact, ridiculing the Real Presence. At the time of the Consecration, the bread and wine were transformed into literal flesh and blood; that is, the Body and Blood of Christ appeared in actual visible form, producing reverence and repentance on the part of the priest. The church holds a Pilgrim Mass each evening.

The cobbled stone streets lead us to our lodging for the night, an old stone building. Our bedroom window opens up on the slanted slate roofs of village houses with a sight of rolling mountains in the distance. The extra-thick walls remind us of the harsh winters this region endures. The room gives off a warm feel, all finished in wood paneling and double windows, rich pink tones and fluffy bed comforters. The indoor window is open for the season and leaves a gap the size of the thickness of the wall for insulation in winter, deep enough to set all our food supplies and more. The bathroom is no bigger than a closet, but has everything we need.

Hungry for a snack, we find a little Celtic bar and sit outside on tree stumps and thick stone slabs, a blink from the Flintstones. Sticking with the local feel, we order Celtic food: Galician lacon, an aged hot ham and country cheese, served with honey smothered over. Not our favorite—but a friendly village dog is delighted to help us finish our plates.

After helping a thirteen-year-old boy reunite with his lost dad, both of them pilgrim bikers who became separated upon entering the village, we saunter across the rest of the village, shop for souvenirs and join the crowded, lively dining room of the hotel. For dinner, we sample a local specialty called caldo gallego, a traditional white bean soup including cabbage and other greens, potato and fatty pork. It's a perfect dish to fight off the winter chill of the region.

Caldo Gallego
Serves: 4-6
Ingredients:

- 1/3 lb. of lima beans
- 1 lb. of potatoes, peeled and quartered
- 1 cabbage, quartered
- 3 small turnips, quartered
- 1 pork bone
- 5 strips of thick bacon
- Salt and Pepper
- Olive oil

Method:
Soak the lima beans in water overnight.
In a sauce pan, combine the lima beans, the bone, the lard, salt and pepper, and cook on low heat for 90 minutes. Add the potatoes.
Once the potatoes are almost cooked, add the cabbage and turnips, and let simmer.
Remove the bacon from the pan; press it with a spatula to release its juice. Return it all, juice and meat, to the pan.
Cook until the potatoes are ready. Let stand for a few minutes and serve very hot.
Serve with thick country bread slices.

*****

Yesterday before entering O'Cebreiro, a sign announced Santiago ninety five miles ahead, a short distance after ambling from village to village through the countryside of Southern France and Northern Spain for more than 870 miles. We are nearing our goal.

Our casual start at 8:30 a.m. is so casual that we take the wrong trail; a mistake well-rewarded by nature's grand beauty. Situated higher than the village, we now have a fantastic view from atop. Furthermore, we witness the close-up flight of a majestic eagle, imposing with its deployed wings, swerving above our heads.

Back on the correct pathway, we continue to ascend. We choose a crest trail to avoid all contact with roads, in contrast with the road choice selected by most other pilgrims.

A stone-carved pilgrim in medieval clothes, fighting forcefully against a raging wind, dominates the area and welcomes pilgrims at the San Roque pass. Taking in the grandeur of our surroundings, we are already sad at the idea that we will have to wait until next year to pursue our route. In a few hours, we will return to the civilized world and its crazy pace.

Hospital de Condesa and San Juan de Padornelo, the last hamlets before Alto de Poio, have existed since medieval times and welcome the pilgrims that traveled in this harsh region. Vestiges of hospitals and chapels can be seen among the couple of inhabited houses that constitute the villages.

The stark beauty of the landscape is impressed in our minds as we arrive at Alto do Poio. The pass, at 4,386 feet, has a hotel-restaurant on one side of the intersection and a snack bar on the other. A marker indicates ninety miles to Santiago. We reach the top at noon, giving us plenty of time to change from hiking clothes to our evening clothes, and grab some lunch at the café on the outdoor terrace before the taxi arrives to drive us to Santiago for our flight back home.

Figure 49: Remote Chapel in the Mountains, near Col San Roque, Galicia

Year Eight

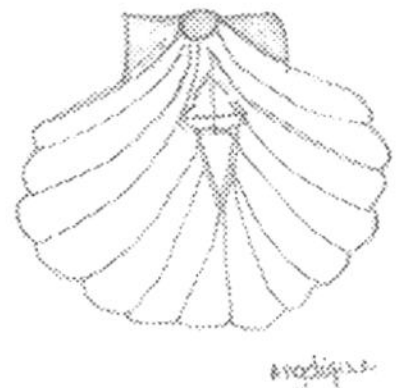

From Alto do Poio to Santiago de Compostella
92 miles in 5 days

"I have fought the good fight, I have finished the race, I have kept the faith."
2 Timothy 4:7

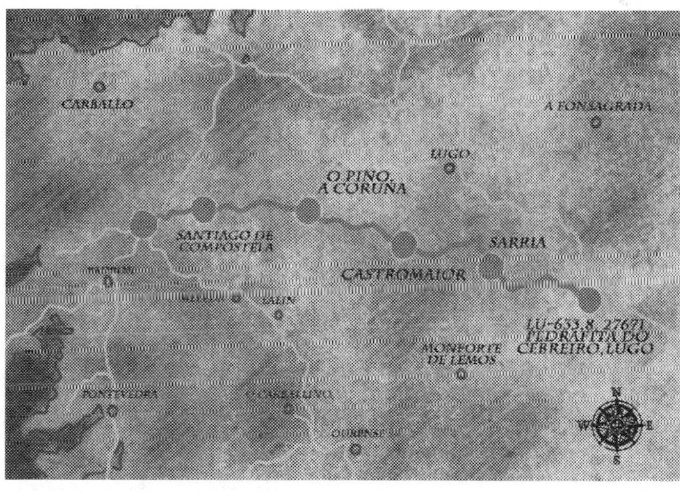

Eight years ago, my mother and I were starting a new adventure, saddened by my uncle's troubles and so virgin at backpacking for long periods of time. Today, we feel like pros; a bit swollen-headed with ourselves that we hardly practice before we depart, only a few walks around the neighborhood, carrying our backpacks.

My arrival in Paris on Thursday morning grants me time to devour an Osso Bucco, prepared by my mom. Mmm—I love French food. Not so rushed with a tight schedule this year, we barely have five days' worth of hiking to reach our final destination. I take the time to eat, shop and soak in the French lifestyle that I miss at times.

Our direct flight to Santiago departs Paris Friday midafternoon. Direct flights to Santiago run only twice a week, so Friday works out perfectly. Just over two hours later, after jabbering nonstop, we land in Galicia, the western tip of Europe.

Our taxi Fermin is waiting to bring us back to the remote region we left a year ago, a pass at 4,400 feet of altitude that is the culminating point of the mountainous chain in Galicia. About two hours later, swerving on narrow roads, we reach Alto do Poio with excitement and anticipation.

We get our bearings and recognize the hotel we left last year as night falls over the pass. Knowing there was only one small hotel here, I had safely made a reservation from Green Bay to secure a room for our late arrival, as well as a late dinner.

The Santa Maria do Poio hotel-restaurant is busy tonight. I make my way to the bar to catch the attention of the bartender. Using my rusty Spanish skills, I manage to inform her that we have a reservation for one bedroom. She seems uneasy while looking at her notebook and lets us know there is no room available. Understanding quite clearly what is happening, my mother's face looks anguished.

I insist that we purposely bothered to call ahead to reserve a room due to our late arrival and the limited options at the pass. Hearing the commotion, the owner emerges from somewhere behind the bar, and after a few inaudible words exchanged with the bartender, he tells us that he does have a room for us. Relieved, we hasten to our room upstairs. We have just enough time to wash our hands and head back downstairs to the dining room, which already is filled with other hikers.

The typical peregrine menu is served: a bowl of rich, wintery vegetable soup followed by fried eggs over sausage or pork chops, and greasy fries, watered down with a house red wine. The owner passes by and my mother, who always thinks she need to add salt to any dish, asks me to request more salt. The innkeeper gives me the evil eye and refuses to hand us some salt, explaining in an irritated tone that the cook has used the necessary amount of salt while cooking. He casually walks away leaving us dumbfounded, torn between laughing and rebellion.

Only a short moment passes and he returns to our table, frowning and unhappy. We wonder what we are up for. Angered, he scolds us about leaving the light on in the bathroom upstairs. A frosted doorway right at the top of the flight of stairs leads to our bedroom, which is adjacent to our bathroom. We label him within the crabby category and move on with our evening.

Back in our room, I crawl in my fluffy blue sleeping bag with my book. This year I invested in a good sleeping bag, extra-light, extra-warm, which can fold as small as a water bottle, knowing that we would be in need of one at some point during the week. I am not willing to spend anymore nights freezing while others are sound asleep.

*****

Good morning and welcome to a rested man! Our gall innkeeper greets us happily from behind the bar and serves us breakfast with a smile—a changed man. An enormous puffy, sugary croissant, so large and sticky that it is served with silverware and hot chocolate.

Leaving the pass on a trail bordered by hilly fields delimited by rusty old barbed wire and white boulders, the sky in front of us is blue with a trail of high altitude clouds painted in light and dark pink tones. We follow the electrical pylons backward down the valley from which they come.

The small, traditional villages of Fonfria, Viduelo and Pasantes are peaceful, built with local stones and slates dotted here and there by little bars. In Pasantes, a baby-blue tray sits on a table in the shade of an umbrella. It holds clear containers filled with a mixture of red currant and blackberries in the courtyard of a home embellished with many potted flowers. A couple of containers are already missing, and upon looking closer, a little round box sits there with an inscription on the lid that says: One Euro Donation. Who could resist! Fresh berries while walking—Yum!

We notice cabbages in large quantities among the regular vegetables growing in the gardens, only they look different than what we are familiar with. Standing hip-high on long, bare stems like flowers, they are striped from the bottom leaves and look a bit peculiar. We find out that in the area, people pick a leaf or two every day for the soupe du jour, a tradition for this remote region characterized by a rustic lifestyle among the mountains.

Figure 50: Cabbages growing - Pick a Leaf or Two a Day to Make the Daily Soup.

The temperature, above normal for the season, reaches eighty-eight degrees during the day. A pleasant, refreshing breeze keeps us comfortable while hiking. We stop for a tea break at the Café-Bar O Peregrino in Triacastela. We sit across the street by a flat stone wall on a bistro-style table topped with a map of the camino frances. It's fun to locate our position and look backward at the distance we have covered. We enjoy naming all the cities and villages we discovered, just like rewinding a movie.

Exiting Triacastela, a tall and thin stone pyramid, adorned with a red metallic sword and capped with a small statue of Saint James, evokes an old tradition in which pilgrims had to load a heavy limestone, extracted from the nearby quarries, in their bag to carry for a day to the ovens of Castaneda. The stones would be transformed into lime and used for the construction of the Basilica of Compostella.

Two options are available from here to reach Sarria, and we opt for our guide's suggestion to follow San Xil, which on top of being closer to the historical tracing, also offers a wider variety of landscapes. Walking along, we are attracted by a strong scent emanating from a building. We peek in to see a young man busy organizing and getting ready for an audience. Chairs are laid out in a semicircle, facing a wicker tall chair. He tells us in a British accent that he plays inspiring music in the afternoons for whoever wants to stop and listen. The strong scent is ever-present and so peaceful. A natural carpet of lavender twigs covers the ground extensively behind the chairs. A real invitation to rest.

The terrain is constantly changing; we are climbing, descending, and meandering from farm to farm, calvaries to chapels, striding across brooks on stone steps, smelling the lush vegetation, the moss, noticing the abundance of chestnut trees. There is a perpetual change of scenery as we continue our descent into the valley. There are no extraordinary monuments to report, but one type of construction worth mentioning is the horreos. These typically long, narrow grain storage units are used to hold and ripen all forms of grain and farm produce, and protect it from moisture and rodents. Corn is the most common crop stored in them, but they can hold just about anything. With the scale of modern agriculture, the horreos are no longer practical nor constructed for farming use anymore. Only the little villages still use them for their personal consumption. Their distinctive appearance, a stony elevated structure, makes them a landmark of northwestern Spain. Traditionally, they are made of granite, elevated on legs, with timber or granite side panels. The roof is usually tiled and there is a small cross at one end. The corn inside is laid out flat in neat rows, stacked up in four or five layers and separated for air circulation.

We find the bar Casa do Franco and its welcoming yard in Furela around lunchtime. We air out our sweaty feet and order inside: a clara and tuna salads, an appetizing plate of tuna, asparagus, tomatoes and beets. It's a pleasant change from the typical prosciutto and cheese sandwich.

Figure 51: Galician Chapel

The bathroom, located on the outside of the restaurant around to the right, has a couple of stalls. Across from the stalls, at eye level, is a little white box attached to the wall with blue, handwritten letters spelling the word *papel* for everyone to see. Woe to the person who enters the stall paperless—one should always carry squares of toilet paper in their pockets in the event of an urgent need. This is a bullet point on our morning checklist—put a few squares of toilet paper in our cargo pants pockets.

After lunch, we inch our way to Sarria following a path bordered by handmade, uneven stone walls used to demarcate the grazing fields from the trails. Modern, hideous, and large, Sarria is a disappointment. We feel like we are arriving through a low-income housing section of town. The buildings, newly built for the most part, are five or six stories high, some bi-color, others sadly painted grey. A corn field stands right in the middle of it all, waiting for a developer to erect another apartment building. Everything is new, even the streets and sidewalks lined with street lights.

There is no hotel in sight, so we keep on moving toward the center of town, climbing uptown, where the historical buildings stand. Still no hotel, only albergues with medium to large dormitories, which is a not-so-appealing idea for tonight. We are very tired for this first extensive day and would like some privacy.

We continue from albergue to albergue, asking for private bedrooms, an occasional luxury offered by some. We are losing hope and starting to picture ourselves settling for the worse when unexpectedly, a manager concerned by our fate tells us to sit right there in the lobby and wait. He makes a call and waves us back to announce that he has found a room for two in town for a modest price. Our bright smiles back, we unload our backpacks and wait, relieved, for he has arranged a car ride for us, since the room is far by foot.

We thank the manager, and when a young lady arrives to pick us up, we board and let her guide us back to the lower part of town, the newer section, on the other side of the river. The parking lot at our destination is very large, unleveled, and not paved. It stretches out in front of a brand new building, four stories high, tan with reddish-brown outdoor blinds. The rooms on the second floor are spotless, small with twin beds, wood floor and bare white walls. The bathroom in the hallway is to be shared with others staying on the same floor.

Waiting in line for the shower, we take turns standing in the hallway while someone, unaware that this is not a private bathroom, indulges in the shower for over twenty minutes. Noticing this issue, the cleaning lady, a funny older woman, knocks on the door to hasten things. A hairy Spanish man soon exits the room with a towel wrapped around his naked body, bare feet, proud of himself, clean and happy. The stereotypical macho man. Only one look in the bathroom and I am turned off.

The floor is inundated from one end to the other and the mirror is all fogged up. There is hair everywhere. Fortunately, the old cleaning lady comes to the rescue. Grumbling in Spanish, she points in his direction and quickly fixes up the bathroom for our use. The beauty of living in shared quarters is still better than sharing sleeping quarters.

After showering, it is time to explore Sarria. The boardwalk edging the river is punctuated with restaurants and cafés. We stop for a drink and tapas, map out our next day's itinerary, write our diaries and people watch. It is Saturday night, and this mid-size town is hopping, filling with locals, starting to invade the outdoor terraces for the evening. The waitress, carrying a large tray, passes around and between tables, offering all sorts of tapas, hot or cold, to share with friends. Children are running loose on the boardwalk while parents socialize. Overly dressed young adults pass by on their way to parties or fancy dinners, maybe a nearby wedding. Laughter and loud voices fill the area, a typical trait of Spain where outdoor life dominates.

We pursue our visit of the town, looking for a café that opens up early enough so we can have breakfast before we leave. Back on the boardwalk, we select an Italian restaurant for dinner only to find out pizzas are lone item on the menu. But we were so hungry for pasta! The Italian chef, not busy yet due to the early hour, agrees to cook a dish of spaghetti Bolognese just for us.

After dinner, we cross the empty field in front of our building, climb the steps to the second floor, and soon crawl to bed for the night. We are brutally awakened around 2 in the morning by a combination of obnoxiously loud people, talking and laughing in the hallways, followed by the backfiring of motorcycles down by the entrance to the building. Irritated, I get up to peek out the window to see what is going on. To my surprise, the lot is jammed full with cars, motorcycles, and people walking to the next door premises, a hidden night club. The party goes on all night, with people entering and exiting the building, thoughtless of who might be sleeping.

At 6:00 a.m. we awaken to the sounds of a couple who had just returned to their room, adjacent to ours, and are sharing their lovemaking with the whole floor. Torn between exasperation and laughter, we slowly get ready to the sound of love. What a night!

*****

Rain is falling steadily this morning, so we slip on our dark green ponchos, dress our backpacks in their waterproof covers, and head out of the building. The town is sleeping and quiet in the dark morning. We amble over the bridge, crossing the Rio Sarria, to catch breakfast when I realize that I am missing by water bottle—darn! I return to the building to look for it and find it in the closet in the room. Those lovers, now sound asleep, had been a source of distraction.

The only open cafe is located in the upper part of town, centered among the *albergues.* It caters to the pilgrims who are up and ready early, either in need of food or to leave their bags for a porterage service. The chairs are still stalked up outside, but the light announces to customers the cafe is already open. A hot beverage and tostadas to start the day and we are off, ready to face the rain.

The streets, paved and wet from the rain, are silent except for the echoes of the metal tips of our hiking sticks as they hit the pavement with every step, helping us climb to exit the town built on a hill. Reaching the top of the hill, we turn around to observe the sleepy town beneath us under a dark, tormented cloudy sky.

With Sarria behind us, we enter a world from the past with medieval bridges and deep, chestnut forests. The minuscule hamlets, connected by rugged paths, bordered by low walls and blackberry bushes, are always so tempting when walking by. We cross brooks on strange, flat flagstone, the *corredoiras,* to keep our feet dry. The countryside looks so much like our French Brittany, the same shades of green and grey, and the same lighting.

Figure 52: The Last 100 Kilometers

The Saint James milestones, placed every 500 meters to announce the final countdown, are thrilling for those eager to finish and devastating for those dreading the end of this adventure. Right around a corner, the 100-kilometer milestone stands there, attired in hundreds of handwritten messages, capped with stones stacked one at a time by pilgrims. This is also the beginning of a new trend: the pilgrims are shedding their hiking sticks, socks, even hiking boots as a testimonial of their passage and the near conclusion of an old life, breaking away from the past to start a new existence.

Encouraging messages are painted on the road as we enter the village of Morgade, where the only café, nestled at the bottom of a stone home, serves all the traffic walking past. The rain has stopped and we can finally drop our ponchos. Sitting outside, we enjoy a hot beverage and a Serrano ham sandwich, served on a half loaf of country bread. Not kidding!

Continuing on, we follow rugged paths and small roads, crossing hamlets sprinkled with small churches and cemeteries. We arrive to a tall wooden cross, planted near a stone wall in the forest. The shedding trend has now fully developed. Strings have been stretched from the cross to the nearby trees to provide hanging space. Everything is there: socks to T-shirts, caps to flags, pinecones to gloves, and many airplane tags. With time, many items have fallen to the ground, and unfortunately the area now looks like a garbage dump.

The road in front of us is clearly marked. There is no need to look for the signs on the walls or around the corners. One only needs to follow the flow of pilgrims. We are getting near, and the increase in the amount of pilgrims is evident.

The big brown cows are coming in for the season, walking in the narrow streets of the villages and witnessing our efforts toward one common goal. Again, a thoughtful soul has left a bowl of apples and tomatoes on a stump, encouraging the tired hikers and inviting us to rest on a bench inside a stone shelter. Leaving a coin or two, we pick a tomato to jazz up our snack of the day.

Figure 53: Help Yourself, Brave Pilgrim

Portomarin is in sight. An old town newly rebuilt, it sits on the top of a hill across from us on the other side of the Rio Mino. The river has a surprisingly large riverbed, yet a very small flow for the season. The medieval town, from the tenth century, was intentionally drowned by the waters of the Rio Mino in the early 1960s after the construction of a dam to create a reservoir for the region. The remnants of the village can be seen near the bottom of the remaining arch from the old bridge. Crossing the new bridge is easier said than done. Aside from the fear of height, we have to brave the forceful wind that shoves us around the narrow path.

Reaching the other side, we can admire all the important buildings that were saved from the swallowing waters and rebuilt stone by stone on the hill in the midst of newly constructed white houses. It is cold and misty, so we decide to eat inside to warm up. The meson Rodrigues in the center of town, a *pulperia*, specializes in serving octopus. It is busy, but we find a seat inside and order a large plate of *pulpo a la gallega*. Served on a wooden plate, it is sliced in pieces half an inch thick, warm and seasoned just right, with olive oil, garlic and hot pepper.

A group of French older women who are traveling with a guided tour and hiking parts of the trail, talk with us for a while comparing their fun at their age to our fun at our age. We finish our lunch with another Galician specialty, the Tarta de Santiago, an almond pie named in honor of Saint James filled with almonds, eggs and sugar. The top of the pie is decorated with powdered sugar depicting the imprint of the Cross of Saint James.

Tarta de Santiago

Serves: 6-8

Ingredients:

- ½ lb. crushed raw almonds
- ½ lb. granulated sugar
- 5 eggs
- 1 lemon, grated
- 1 Tbs. powdered sugar to sprinkle
- 1 Tb. salted butter to spread on the mold
- 1/2 tsp. powdered cinnamon
- 1 8-inch round detachable mold

Method:

Preheat the oven at 350° F.

In a bowl, combine the sugar, the crushed almonds, the cinnamon and the lemon zest. Mix well.

Add the eggs and blend all ingredients gently.
Spread the butter on the mold and pour the mix in it.
Place in the oven for 45-50 minutes until the surface is golden. The cake is done if a toothpick inserted into the center of the cake comes out clean.
Cool briefly and remove the cake from the pan. When the cake has cooled down, sprinkle the top with powdered sugar after placing a 4-inch Cross of Santiago in the center. You can also use a cut-out of the sword of St. James.

We brave the rain and gusting wind pushing us sideways for two hours. Covered in green from head to toe with our fancy ponchos, we blend in with the lush bushes and forests. The road, never too far, is not bothersome, hiding and popping in and out at times. The albergue in Gonzar is full, so we continue our route to Castromaior, half a mile away. The village is soundless and empty throughout its length. We do find a room on the main strip right in the center of the village. The white house is lined with dark red borders and kept up by an older woman. The facility is clean and we have a private bathroom, which is a luxury at this late hour. The other bedrooms have to share a common bathroom.

The village is deserted in appearance only. We find out that the villagers are celebrating a local feast and are spending time with their family at home. The only chance for us to eat was the one and only bar which is closed. Walking through the village on the cobblestone main street, we run into the bar owner. She is aware of our desperate need for food and offers to prepare dinner and have it ready at 7:00 p.m. She lists a few options right here, orally, in the middle of the street. We agree upon a menu: lentil soup to start, tortilla de asparagus with fries for main course. Perfect, we are in! With the limited options we have tonight, we are glad to eat whatever she will serve us. There is no room for picky eaters tonight.

Cleaned up early, we go to the bar and join other hikers who have gathered to have a drink and olives. The bar owner is cooking and has already set the tables for all of us.

*****

Up at 6:45 a.m., we wake to find our gear still wet from yesterday. The room is cold, not heated at all, and damp. It rained all night and we can feel the humidity coming out of the thick walls. We get out our spare gear and prepare for the day.

We hustle to the café, which is supposed to open at 7:30 a.m. for breakfast. The village is asleep in the dark morning. The villagers must have partied very late, and to our dismay, the cafe is still closed when we arrive. There is no light, not a soul, and our empty stomachs ache.

A group of hikers coming from the albergue in Gonzar is using headlights to light up the way, so we decide to follow them. Forty minutes later, we reach a hamlet with an open café. It is now daytime and also rush hour among hikers. The joint is packed! We find a free corner around the bar and order hot cafe latte, served in tall and thick glasses, with morning pastries. The bartender is overwhelmed with the unexpected crowd and the endless wait is frustrating.

The rain is still coming down, but the wind has calmed. We cross many tranquil hamlets and sense the Galician influence in every house. The cows, clothed in deep caramel dresses, look at us like we are odd creatures with deformed bodies. They are living among the villagers in the lower part of their farm houses in the center of the villages. Looking at each other, we understand their puzzled faces: two hunter-green, hooded hunchbacks staring back at them. If only they could talk. We can only imagine their sarcastic comments, a smile on their face.

Depleted of picnic provisions, we unearth a couple of chocolate squares from a bar brought from France to share on the side of the road, across from another closed restaurant that has shut down for the season.

The end is near and the grueling mental effort can be more demanding than the strenuous physical one. After Brea, we come upon two ladies, hiker companions, who are stopped on the side of the road. One is waiting for the other who, out of despair, has thrown her hiking stick in the ditch. Pain, fatigue, mental exhaustion, whatever her setback is, she has reached her limit for the day. This can explain why many people have made the choice to hike alone at their own pace, not having to worry about a companion's mental or physical state.

Around lunch time, we happily reach a larger town, Palas de Rei. The town has a good selection of restaurants and cafes, just in time to fill our growling stomachs. A foot-long sandwich cut in half, filled with prosciutto and tomatoes, hits the spot and brings content smiles to our tired faces. The young couple ensconced at a table behind amazes us with their determination. They are hiking the St James way with one large backpack and their baby, in a carrier on Mom's back. How brave!

The afternoon is wet and features the same decor as this morning, serpenting in the Galician countryside through medieval hamlets. We arrive in O Coto for teatime to find an open tavern. Due to the rain, the majority of the customers are crammed inside in a small cacophonous room. A few of us escape the commotion to find peace outside under a wide, sheltering tree on the outdoor terrace. A few drops falling here and there does not phase our easygoing mind. Only a couple of adjustments needed to stay dry takes care of it.

Roman bridges, purple heather and yellow broom, hamlets, and small churches with flat steeples punctuate the rest of the day until we discern the sketch of modern buildings, colorful like a patchwork of habitations. The scenery is not so pleasant as we near the outskirts of Melide. There is a feeling of poverty resonating through the unfinished apartment buildings. The Carlos Hotel, suggested in our guide, is located on the main road.

Cleaned up but stranded indoors due to the rain, we decide to indulge in the bathtub for a long, warm repairing bath. Dinner is served after 8:30 p.m. and the entire hotel is gathered in the bar, drinking and snacking, in wait of the service. Cauliflower soup and cooked tongue are on the menu—very mediocre. Finally fed, we return to our room after jabbering with Canadians and French hikers and bikers.

The night is interrupted again by some rowdy hotel guests.

*****

After a copious breakfast with cheese, ham, bread and the whole buffet, we leave the hotel on a cloudy and rainy morning. The gear dried well last night in the hotel, and we slip into our green ponchos to start the day's hike. At the exit of Melide, the marker K. 50 with the yellow shell presiding on top encourages the hikers on their last stretch; two days tops.

We then enter the forests of eucalyptus, somber and dense. The size of these trees is impressive, so high that you have to stop to look for the top branches. The ground is covered with thin, pinkish bark that fell from the eucalyptus trunks as if they were shedding. The strong smell, enhanced by the rainy day, is unique and very enjoyable.

Horses and cows are back in the décor as we are in the plains again. A cow gives birth to a calf in the field all by herself, with no supervision, the umbilical cord still hanging there. We look at him with amazement as he barely stands on his legs.

The proximity of Santiago is perceptible! All around us, people are converging toward a common objective. Some are hardcore hikers like us, some are hikers for the day, torn between living the real thing and struggling with giving up wearing a sexy green mini-skirt, shawl and sparkly white tennis shoes, walking hand in hand, in love, still living the 1960s.

The rain has not stopped and the capes are holding up very well. An hour stop is needed in Ribadiso de Baixo, a charming village restored all in stone with red tile roofs and light blue windows.

The rain is still coming down when we arrive in Arzua, a larger town with sidewalks and street lights. The ongoing drizzle falls from the pale white sky. A blessed soul has set up a food stand, buffet-style, inviting pilgrims to rest and have a bite. Fresh fruits, homemade baked breads and cookies, and hot or cold beverages. Only a mere request posted on the welcoming sign suggests leaving a donation in the box. A letter revealing the history of the house describes how the present owners, a couple who hiked the trail themselves, had noticed the house and ended up buying it. After restoring it, they cultivated the goal of setting up an organic farm, raising sheep, chickens and geese, and of course, always providing fresh fruits for hikers. Along with a handy, precise description of the next eighteen miles, a word of encouragement completes the letter and puts us back on the road.

Shortly after, we arrive in Calle, a small village, deserted with narrow, winding streets, low slate roofs, and large, uneven stone houses, and find a café for a dry break.

The rain has not stopped and it is necessary to warm up and dry off a bit. The long wooden table, surrounded by benches, fills the space in the small long room. To the left, a few shelves against the wall are stocked with a selection of fruits, chips and other snack options. The lady owner, standing behind her counter, takes our order of claras and chips, but soon we are hungry again and beg for a tuna salad. Meanwhile, a couple from Israel comes in, soaked as well. They left three weeks ago from the French border on bikes with a little trailer to carry their baby. How courageous! The baby, enjoying the trip, is smiling and happy to get out and play. Next, a Frenchman arrives as we are getting ready to leave. Drenched and looking miserable, this high-spirited fellow calmly claims to our dismay, "This is only water!"

Six miles yet before the night stop, and the sky does not show any hope for a sunny spell ahead. The rain pelts down and keeps us moving quickly through more eucalyptus forests, where strong, wet scents invade my nostrils and makes up for this wet day. Muddy trails, dark and lost in the deep woods, flow through a succession of forests.

As we near the end of the day, we rely more and more on the markers indicating the distance to cover. However, we also notice, as it is mentioned in our guidebook, that the markers are not very reliable in this region. Some portions seem to last forever while others are startlingly short.

We call ahead to make a reservation at the Casa Rural de Rua to secure a room for our late arrival. Approaching Rua, we notice a sign posted on the front door of an albergue stating they are full. We congratulate each other for our early initiative. Arriving in front of our lodging, two ladies, hiking partners, come out of the lobby area. They are a bit stressed out after unsuccessfully searching for a room to sleep in. Our casa rural is full, too! At this late hour, no one wants to add any more miles to an already long day to find lodging. Planning ahead as we get closer to Santiago is definitely necessary.

The place is charming, with a pool and lawn chairs ready for us in the beautiful yard. If only the weather was cooperating! Our room, located in the back of the property, faces the pool and is set in a small construction similar to a bungalow. It accommodates two separate rooms with patio doors, opening onto a furnished terrace. The room, decorated in orange and offset with blue tones, is warm and inviting.

Tonight again, we are forced to stay inside due to the sad weather. We decide once again to indulge in a bath while waiting for dinner. After stuffing our hiking boots with newspaper borrowed at the front desk, hoping to remove the excess of moisture, we join the guests in the dining room for supper. The room is full and jovial, as many pilgrims share their daytime stories. As we sit down, we notice a collection of coins from around the world that people have left behind as a token of their passage, laying them on stones protruding from the wall. Original and catchy, we are also drawn by the idea and happily contribute to the tradition by leaving a French coin and an American coin. The thirteen euro menu for pilgrims is quite tasty, starting with lentil soup followed by a paella dish.

*****

I start the morning with a glass of hot chocolate and grilled country bread with butter and jelly. Today is the day—we are going to make it to Santiago. Unbelievable!

Figure 54: Santiago: City Limit Sign

Our shoes are not dry and the sky, rather dark, releases more rain here and there. The trail is a little bit busy, but nothing like we were picturing on this last portion.

The last thirteen miles are full of surprises, such as spontaneous love letters written on a wall, and a pair of hiking boots and a belt abandoned on a marker. People are sensing the end drawing near and feel the need to leave traces of their passage, to be ready to embrace a new beginning once there, to express their feelings.

The sky is dark, the sun is out; the mix of emotion is in the air! The end means so many things in so many ways. Ending a long route also implies a return to civilization. The noise of the city is becoming more prominent with cars, airplanes, children going to school, and as a real eye-opener, the airport sits astride our route for a while.

A stele with a large scallop shell and a hiking stick announces the entrance of the Santiago suburb. In Lavacolla, the last village before the city, pilgrims used to clean up, organize their belongings, and prepare to honor St James. As a wink to our ancestors, we make one last symbolic stop before reaching the cathedral. The cafe we stop at is packed, partly due to the rain. We recognize more and more people that we have seen along the way, all funneling to the cathedral.

Only six and a half miles to go, over many unexpected hills. The backpacks are feeling strangely heavy after this short morning. Our heads have already arrived.

Later, we reach another landmark, a modern monument at the Gozo Mount where we catch the first glimpse in the distance of the cathedral towers in Santiago. It is here that in 1989, Pope John Paul II gathered 5,000 youths. Many pilgrims are here taking pictures and looking at the view of the city finally lying in front of them. The albergue of Santiago is located nearby on the way down from the mount. The place is closed at this hour, but we can see it is massive. It is ready to host as many as 2,000 pilgrims at once, which we hear is barely enough room on busy days. Four large steps give way to a large alleyway lined with young trees on each side, tables and chairs, and benches leading to rooms on the outside of the esplanade. Only three more miles before we reach the cathedral!

So begins the crossing of Santiago de Compostela, a modern town, through busy streets, walking on sidewalks, looking at the daily life of this mystic city at the far west end of the Iberian peninsula. Eager to arrive, the crossing seems endless. We look for clues of the cathedral at each corner.

Meandering through the new town, we finally reach the old town, where the cathedral is centrally located. Santiago is opening its doors to us. The city is like a hive of activities with accomplished pilgrims everywhere, smiling, content, and peaceful.

Others like us are still in quest of the final landmark, the cathedral. Freshly arrived and looking like it, we are approached by many individuals who are offering rooms for the night. Santiago is packed and we start wondering about our lodging options. But first we must find the cathedral.

Unexpectedly, it appears to our left, and after stepping down a few steps covered by a porch, where a woman dressed in Galician attire plays the bagpipes, we set foot on the well-known plaza del Obradoiro. The mile zero of the Saint James Way, located in the center of this square, concludes our pilgrimage. We made it! Eight years of persistence to achieve a dream.

The entrance to the majestic cathedral is so massive that we need to walk to the opposite side of the plaza to embrace the dimension of the edifice. A stone bench framing the right side of the place makes a perfect observational position. We feel a mixture of pride for accomplishing such a rewarding adventure, but also a bittersweet sensation that something unique has just ended.

Figure 55: Facing the Cathedral in Santiago after Eight Years of Perseverance! Plaza de Obradoiro

Scattered puddles are still covering the paved plaza, but just like a graduation gift, the sun is peering through a few white clouds, allowing for a time of rest and contemplation. The place is surrounded by inspiring buildings: the cathedral, the hotel de ville and the palatial Parador.

We settle on the weathered stone bench, bathed in bright sun, remove our shoes, curl up and take it all in–the cathedral, the people, reflecting on our voyage.

The Plaza del Obradoiro shows Santiago in its entire splendor. It is like an architectural catalogue: Romanesque art in the Colegio de San Xerome, the head office of the University of Santiago de Compostela; Baroque style in the cathedral façade, with the museum at its right and the Gelmírez Palace at its left; Neo-Classic style in the Palacio de Raxoi, which serves as the current city hall; and lastly, Plateresque art demonstrated in the old pilgrims' hospital, now a five-star hotel—the Hostal de los Reyes Católicos. In keeping with its tradition, the Hostal provides breakfast, lunch and dinner free of charge to the first ten pilgrims to arrive at its door every day with their Compostela to prove that they have covered at least the last one hundred kilometers (equivalent to sixty-two miles) on foot.

Recovering from our first emotions, we notice that our stomachs are screaming for fuel. After all, it is past 2:00 p.m. An express restaurant, connected to the Parador, on the plaza tempts us. The decor is Parador-like, elaborate, and filled with tourists fancily dressed to visit the holy city. The specialty of the month suggestion—prawns and octopus served with Garbanzo beans—is overrated and a disappointment. How much more touristy does it get? What did we expect?

By the end of our lunch, the sky has changed from a pale blue, filtered sun through light, sparse clouds to a down pouring rain.

This is when we start our quest for a hotel in the historical center of Santiago. The first hotel we try is full and so is the second. Homeless and at the mercy of the wet weather, an uneasy feeling settles in. Santiago is swarming with tourists, hikers, pilgrims and guided tours. The city offers a vast selection of lodging of all sorts, but what if? We should have made a reservation despite the long list of accommodations listed.

It is time to react and take action. We look for a dry spot, pull out our hotel list for Santiago and start calling one at a time. A four-star hotel, the Pousadas de Compostella, has a room available. The price is a little elevated, but we feel we deserve a treat, a sort of graduation gift. After deciphering the Spanish direction over the phone from the hotel clerk, we set off for the hotel, walking along the walls through the narrow streets, and avoiding the rain as much as possible.

The hotel is only a five-minute walk from the cathedral, across from the famous covered farmers market. The four stars are well worth it. Right here in the middle of the city, the hotel has a unique situation. To reach our room, we exit the lounge in the back of the hotel and walk along a manicured garden decorated with statues, trees and flowers on a covered path. Our room, on the first floor, opens up onto the garden, where lush lawn appeases the eye. The suite is spacious yet cozy, with warm colors and snug furniture. It is our end of the trip present.

We stay in our hiking gear, leave our packs in the suite, and head for the cathedral to validate our credentials. A few familiar pilgrims are in search of the office as well, and after looking at maps together, we find the pilgrims office a couple of streets away.

A line of pilgrims in the courtyard, all eager to get the famous paper justifying the efforts they all went through, extends from the street to the entrance to a staircase in an inside courtyard. While waiting for over thirty minutes, we proceed to create a detailed analysis of all the pilgrims in line. Who is who? Where do they come from? How far did they really walk? Who do we know?

After climbing the stairs, we arrive in a small room that leads to individual booths for a private interview in Spanish. Our apprehension level rises as we wait for our turn, just like the old school days on your way to an oral exam. Our interviewers, next to each other, begin the official inspection and interview. A series of question begins.

"Where did you start the pilgrimage?" says the female clerk.

"In the Puy en Velay, in France" I shyly answer.

"What have been the stages you stopped at in the last one hundred kilometers?" she continues.

Unable to think of the names of the last few cities we crossed, I stumble over my words looking for what to say in Spanish. Just like a test fright!

My interviewer inspects my credential and starts frowning upon looking at it. Worried, I whisper a "What's the matter?" and to my great surprise, she tells me that I should have had my credential stamped twice a day over the last one hundred miles, a measure needed to deter people from cheating. Uneasy for a moment, she scolds me a bit and hands me a form to fill out with standard information such as first and last name, sex, age, nationality, city of residency, profession and motivational reasons, whether religious or other.

Finally, she hands me a certificate, rolled in a tube as a scroll and written in Latin, and proceeds to congratulate me for my wonderful accomplishment. Certificate in hand, we proudly descend the staircase, still full of people looking envious and eager to get theirs.

Next, we hop on the tourist train, stationed on the plaza in front the cathedral, for an hour tour of the historical center and the university campus, with English and Spanish commentaries. It is a great way to get a visual of this large city in a flash.

CAPITULUM hujus Almae Apostolicae et Metropolitanae Ecclesiae Compostellanae sigilli Altaris Beati Jacobi Apostoli custos, ut omnibus Fidelibus et Peregrinis ex toto terrarum Orbe, devotionis affectu vel voti causa, ad limina Apostoli Nostri Hispaniarum Patroni ac Tutelaris **SANCTI JACOBI** convenientibus, authenticas visitationis litteras expediat, omnibus et singulis praesentes inspecturis, notum facit:

hoc sacratissimum Templum pietatis causa devote visitasse. In quorum fidem praesentes litteras, sigillo ejusdem Sanctae Ecclesiae munitas, ei confero.

Datum Compostellae die 26 mensis Septembris anno Dni 2012.

Canonicus Deputatus pro Peregrinis

Upon our return, we walk back to the hotel for a warm bath and a well-deserved rest. At eight, we enjoy a *Pacharan* and olives in the hotel lounge while talking to the bartender about the origin of the Pacharan. He proceeds to tell us that here in Galicia, people tend to order a glass of wine or a beer before their meal instead of a liquor.

The dining room, located in the back corner of the garden, is half full when we arrive for dinner. The menu is appealing and we order red peppers stuffed with crab, and creamy *bacalao*, a cod specialty. The food is excellent and the service is perfect, even though the waiters have to run back and forth from the "outdoor" dining room to the kitchen in the main part of the hotel.

*****

Such an adventure cannot end here, right now, so quickly … no backpack, no mileage to count and recount, no day map to examine the next morning at breakfast. So we get up, indulge in a royal breakfast, where a large buffet offers fresh juices, pastries, ham, cheese and more, and cross the road to take a tour of the market, "el Mercado de Abastos," located a few steps behind the cathedral. The fresh food market has been open since 1873, offering a wide variety of locally grown vegetables, meat, fish and seafood.

Brandada de bacalao

Serves: 2-3

Ingredients:

- 1 lb. salted cod fillet, soaked, drained and boned
- 9 fl. oz. olive oil
- 7 fl. oz. warm whole milk
- 3 garlic cloves
- 1 bay leaf
- Juice of a small lemon

Method:

Heat the olive oil in a small pan.

Add the milk, bay leaf and garlic in another small pan and heat until warm. Set aside.

Meanwhile, gently poach the cod in cold water, not letting it reach boiling temperature. Set aside for a few minutes.

Remove the skin and any bones and place in a food processor. Add the olive oil and the flavored milk, and process until you obtain a thick paste. Add the lemon juice and serve. Serve with a side of peeled, boiled potatoes, roughly mashed

At 9:15 a.m. we board a cab and head out to the bus station, where we buy two return tickets to Finisterre, known as the end of the earth. In the times of the Romans and Celts, Finisterre was considered to be at the farthest edge of the northwesterly land mass. It was described as "the end of the earth." In Latin, "finis terrae" means "end of the world."

The white and yellow coach bus crosses many little villages in the mountains, stopping in each to pick up or drop off mostly elderly inhabitants. Nauseated from motion sickness, I dose off to ignore the constant curves, accelerations and decelerations of the bus swerving on the mountainous roads at high speed. The landscape changes upon reaching Noio, leaving the mountains to flatter lands. With the ocean to our left, we follow the coast for over an hour, discovering this remote area. The scenery is a mixture of warm climate and mountainous climate, where palm trees, citrus trees and high altitude pine trees share grounds. The, thick, stone habitations are definitely built to cope with the harsh weather.

Forty-five minutes behind schedule, living the Spanish lifestyle, we finally end up in Finisterre for lunch. Where Finisterre does score points is in the portside cafe bars that serve the freshest seafood. These bars are nothing special to look at and most tourists will dismiss them without a second look, but this is their loss. We sit at a restaurant overlooking the harbor to try the famed local seafood. Enjoying our relaxing time, we talk about the options of returning to Santiago on the last bus tonight or staying here overnight. The restaurant owner, happy to use the little bit of French he knows, talks to us and suggests a small hotel in the old part of town, facing the beach with private bath. Tempted, we jump in and let him call in a reservation for us. Shortly after we are finished eating, a young man guides us through the meandering narrow streets of the village, up and down steps, taking short cuts and crossing little squares to arrive to our hotel, Casa Velay, facing the beach indeed. Climbing two floors, we settle in our small room, with a mini bathroom.

Hiking boots on, we set out to the end of the world, the Faro de Fisterra. We follow the paved road for about one and a half miles to the end of the Cape. The renowned lighthouse at Faro de Fisterra was built in 1853 and can be seen on a clear day from eighteen miles at sea. The coastline is rough, jagged, and treacherous.

Fisterra has acquired a reputation for being on "the coast of death," since many vessels have left the port, never to return. Numerous vessels are resting on the floor of the Atlantic, with many more lives lost. It's not only pleasure and fishing boats that run into trouble, but well-documented naval battles between the French and English took place just off Cape Fisterra.

The moment is indelible. We arrive here full of emotions, grateful that the journey is over, even though all know that once you begin walking the Camino, the journey never ends. A hotel, the lighthouse and a couple of touristy shops summarize the extent of what stands here. But more meaningful is the end tip of the peninsula. The large rock is taken over by pensive hikers, staring at the dark blue immensity lying at their feet. The Atlantic Ocean, vast and intimidating, touches the coast of America on the other side.

Nearby is a fire pit where pilgrims offer up a piece of clothing to be burned as a ritual in the sense that the ending of their Camino is part of a new beginning of life. Adjacent to the fire pit a bronzed boot, also a symbol of the end of this part of our journey, is inspiring to all pilgrims. Some sacrifice the worn boots to the fire pit as a significant way to turn the page and embrace their new life. It is a way to get rid of old sufferings, physical and mental, during, and for many pilgrims, before the journey.

The site is stunning. The sun did not miss the rendezvous and it is magical to be here at the end of the world, sitting up high on a boulder facing the ocean, an element that talks to me with so much power through all my senses.

Since we're not into burning our belongings, we enjoy a long hour basking in the sun until the wind, growing stronger, dislodges us from our promontory. Not ready to head back to town yet, we try to hang on as long as we can to this memorable setting. We prolong our pleasure at the outdoor terrace of the tiny hotel Semaphore for one last moment in this remote land.

Figure 56: Faro de Fisterra, the End of the World!

Returning to Finisterre for the evening, we arrive with the fishermen, who are unloading their boats of baskets full of squids and many fish. The harbor is filled with bright, colorful fishing boats, parked behind the pier in the protective harbor. The seagulls and the crowd come to watch the arrival and inspect the catch. We enjoy our last night of an eight-year-long journey with a drink and local munchies on the harbor, protected from the cool wind.

The hotel is very quiet, and after resting in our room, we make our way down to the dining room on the second floor. The room is dark and no one is here. We turn on the light and hope that the chef did not forget about us. The dining room, large and surrounded by windows overlooking the ocean, is pleasant but too quiet tonight. The chef arrives and offers a limited selection of dishes based on the daily seafood arrival. We pick, based on his advice, the stuffed squids cooked in a red wine sauce. It's always a safe idea to follow the advice of the chef in a small and quiet restaurant. Great choice! The food is excellent.

*****

The foghorn awakens us early in the morning, and we get up to catch our bus back to Santiago. It is still dark out when we leave the hotel with all our gear, and the wind has not died down. We cut through the interior of the village, avoiding the coast where the wind whistles this early morning. Across from the bus stop, a bar is open to welcome the travelers. We manage to find a table to share to eat breakfast.

Back in Santiago mid-morning, we head for the cathedral to attend the well-known 12 o'clock Friday Mass. Forty-five minutes early, we are stunned to see how packed the cathedral already is. The immense cathedral used to welcome many is filling up patiently. The seats in the main aisles are occupied and we are lucky to find a seat on a bench near the altar, along the wall to the side. Little by little, the aisle of the cathedral crowds up with groups and individuals of all ages, from kids on school trips to adults. Families, school-age groups and individuals walk as far as permitted and sit down right where they are on the floor in the aisles, leaving a narrow bare path for the procession of priests to walk to the altar. The cathedral is jammed, an unbelievable sight! The Mass lasts about an hour, focused on the pilgrims, mentioning how many pilgrims finished their journey this week, specifically stating each country of origin.

The tradition of burning incense in a swinging censer began in the eleventh century when arriving pilgrims were tired and unwashed. It was also believed that incense smoke had a prophylactic effect in the time of plagues and epidemics.

Of course, incense burning is also an important part of the liturgy.

The Santiago de Compostela Botafumeiro, a swinging metal container, is one of the largest censers in the world, weighing 176 pounds and measuring five feet two inches in height. It is normally on exhibition in the library of the cathedral, but during certain important religious occasions, it is brought to the floor of the cathedral and attached to ropes hung from the pulley mechanism.

The censer is pushed initially to start its motion by eight red-robed *tiraboleiros* who pull the ropes, producing increasingly large oscillations of the censer. The turible's swing almost reaches the ceiling of the transept. The incensory can reach speeds of forty-two miles per hour as it dispenses thick clouds of incense, which infuses the whole edifice. Mesmerized by this spectacle, we realize how lucky we are to witness this ceremony. Once over, the attendants scatter and we start our visit of the majestic structure.

Despite its Baroque façade, the present cathedral of Santiago de Compostela is predominantly Romanesque. The construction began in 1060 in the reign of Alfonso VI and was completed in 1211. The remains of Saint

James, the raison d'être of the cathedral, were lost in 1700 after being hidden before an English invasion. Fortunately, they were rediscovered during some construction work in 1879. The sacred relics of Saint James lay beneath the cathedral's high altar in a silver coffer and can be viewed from the crypt.

After our tour, we head out to Rua Franco, adjacent to the cathedral, where many restaurants populate both sides of the street. It is a definite must-see at night. Most menus posted on the outside mainly list seafood dishes. We order our last pulpo a la gallega and venture to try razor clams, a long shellfish resembling a knife, sautéed in garlic and parsley, and served in the shell for appetizer. I used to collect them on the beach in Normandy when I was a little girl, but have never sampled one. I find them quite tasty! To conclude our gastronomic meal, we stick with the local specialty and order a *tarta* de Compostela.

To celebrate the ending of our voyage, we both buy a silver scallop shell pendant as a symbol to remember the bonding experience that connected us, daughter and mother, during eight consecutive years through this unique adventure.

Epilogue

With many free hours, walking in nature and surrounded by inspiring scenery, I discovered contemplative prayers—a discipline that taught me to be still, slow down, and listen to God's plan for me. Taking the time to listen to him meant reaching deep inside and opening my heart to a higher power. This spiritual enlightenment has come home with me. I find it tremendously uplifting to carve out some time daily to be still and listen!

Of course, it is more challenging to apply this concept to my daily life. The visual noises we are faced with continuously are a major distraction. It can even become comforting to always have some background noise, as if silence is awkward.

Silence can indeed be very rejuvenating. After spending hours with my mother on trails, we both naturally would settle in a contemplation mode, observing, listening and deepening our thoughts to some form of meditation.

The St. James's Way has the power to change anyone who ambles on its trails. Reflecting on this journey has piqued my interest on how the trail might alter someone's life. The experiences one encounters on the path have the capability to instill the mindsets and habits of the world's most successful men. The Camino will change you, in a good way, for a better you, for a better life.

Anyone who wants a different harvest in their life has to change what they sow. Imagine a ship without a destination! When a ship leaves port, it has a captain and a roadmap, a destination. The same way the captain set the path for his boat, we have to create our path; we have to be the creators of our life.

Start with a dream! I started with the vision of a heroic epic across an unknown, distant land. Then I laid out the roadmap and focused on my dream. The roadblocks, whatever they might be, cannot stop you before you start any adventure. If they materialize, they will be addressed at that point in time. Fear of what might happen should not prevent anyone from living their dream.

Finally comes the time to take action and step out of our own comfort zone to take the risk and embark on an incredible journey, to challenge ourselves. Once you have crossed the line, bought your ticket, your gear, practiced and boarded your airplane to fly to your final destination, your mixed emotions are ever so present. The excitement prevails over concerns for a while until the worries creep up to take over the joyous moment. And even though you are not sure if this is a good idea, you finally arrive there in front of the first marker pointing in the direction of Santiago.

From this point on, the futile exigencies of the modern world fade away to give way to the daily necessities of this temporary life. A survival mindset settles in, focusing on basic needs that any human takes for granted nowadays, but not so on the trail. Shelter, food and water, clothing, and health will become one's main focus.

Unless these aspects of life are fulfilled, one cannot enjoy life fully. This is indeed true on the trail and back home, too. The difference is that at home our focus is set on fashion, fitting in, what someone will think about someone else, and having all the toys the neighbor has.

Figure 57: My Hiking Boots after 1,000 Miles

Then will come the time when the pilgrim needs to keep a positive attitude while facing complications. You have to use all the resources you have to keep moving forward. Whether in pain, hungry, thirsty, or worried, you have to believe in yourself and find that inner strength you did not know you had.

And last but not least, you open the door to others to come in to share your emotions, joys and hike a while together. There comes a moment for truth, fairness, where no games are played, just pilgrims in the same boat, where differences are neither revealed nor interesting.

The Camino is a life lesson showing you the way on how to run your life, how to accomplish the old buried projects never uncovered, never attempted, that lay at the bottom of your heart for fear of failing, of disappointment, or change.

If you only would give it a chance, all you have to do is follow these five steps in every aspect of your life:

- Start dreaming
- Live a healthy life that meets your basic personal needs
- Take risks and step out of your comfort zone
- Think positive, believe in yourself, and never give up
- Open the door to others, welcome ideas, reach out, and surround yourself with the right people for you.

To my family and friends,

It's hard to believe that this is my final page in the telling of this great adventure. These past few years have been a whirlwind of exciting change and positive developments in my personal life, and thanks to all my supporters I am only continuing to head upward through spiritual experience like this, eager to share with fellow readers. It has been an honor to walk this medieval trail, and I want to thank everyone for their steadfast support throughout this peregrination during which I found inspiration in each day. I consider my time on the Camino to have been extremely rewarding, and I owe much of that to all my family and friends.

Although I'm signing off as a pilgrim, this isn't a goodbye. I'll still be very much involved in sharing more trail discovery in Europe, and I look forward to assisting any potential pilgrims as they plan their new adventure.

I'm grateful that I was entrusted to pursue this adventure over eight years, and I feel strongly that the benefits that grew out of it will benefit many in their mission of reaching a better life through positive attitude, spirituality, positive relationships and healthy lifestyle.

Once again, thank you to all my family and friends. It has been a pleasure to share this immense experience.

Glossary

French – English

Aligot - Mashed Potatoes with Garlic and Cheese

Auberge - Inn

Bienvenue, gardez le moral - Welcome, Keep Your Spirits Up

Bordelais - From the Bordeaux Region

Bourdon - A pilgrim's staff used by pilgrims on the Way of St. James

Caselle - Hut of shepherd

Causse - Limestone plateau

Cèpes - Porcinis

Chausson aux pommes - Apple turnover

Chemin - Path, way

Chien de montagne - Mountain dog

Colombage - Half-timbered

Confit - Duck or other meat cooked slowly in its own fat.

Coulemelle - Parasol mushroom, so called because they look like little umbrellas.

Crème Brulée - Classic French dessert consisting of custard topped with caramelized sugar

Foie Gras - This French delicacy is made of the liver of a duck or goose that has been specially fattened.

Gare - Train station

Gite - Holiday cottage, lodge, shelter

Hors piste - Off-piste

Iles flottantes - Puffy clouds of softly poached meringue floating on a vanilla custard sauce

Logis de France - An organization of smaller hotels which are almost always connected to a fine restaurant.

Menthe à l'eau - Mint Soda

Palombes - Wood Pigeon

Panaché - Shandy

Pastis - Anise-flavored alcohol very popular in the south of France.

Rillettes - Rustic pâté made from meat that's been poached in its own fat, then shredded and stored in some of that fat

Saussison - Dry-cured sausage

Spanish - English

Albergue - shelter, refuge, lodging

Ayuntamiento - city hall

Bacalao - cod fish

Calle - street, road

Camino - road, way, path

Clarita - (cerveza con gaseosa) shandy; lager shandy

Corridas - bullfights

Grelos - turnip tops

Horreos - raised granary typical of Asturias and Galicia

Hostal - cheap hotel; boarding house

Hosteria - inn; hostelry

Iglesia - church

Lomo - pork loin

Mercado - market

Meseta - tableland; plateau

Pacharan - Spanish liqueur which is made from crushed and fermented sloes, the black-purple colored fruits of the blackthorn tree

Panaderia - bakery

Papel - paper

Parador - state-owned luxury hotel, often in a building of historic or artistic importance

Pelota - ball

Peregrinos - pilgrims

Pimientos - peppers

Pintxos, Pinchos - tapas

Puente - bridge

Pulpo - octopus

Rio - river

Sangre - blood

Tapas - small portion of food

Tienda - (the) store

Tortilla de patatas - Spanish potato omelet

Tortilla Espanola - Spanish omelet

Tostas - grilled bread

Bibliography

Topo-Guide GR 65 – Sentier de Saint-Jacques-de-Compostelle – Le Chemin du Puy

Le Puy – Aubrac – Conques – Figeac
Fédération Française de la Randonnée Pédestre – FFRP

Topo-Guide GR 65 – Sentier de Saint-Jacques-de-Compostelle – Le Chemin du Puy

Figeac – Cahors – Agen - Moissac
Fédération Française de la Randonnée Pédestre – FFRP

Topo-Guide GR 65 – Sentier de Saint-Jacques-de-Compostelle – Le Chemin du Puy

Moissac – Condom - Ronceveaux
Fédération Française de la Randonnée Pédestre – FFRP

Chemins de Saint-Jacques – Des chemins et leur mémoire à découvrir et à partager

Guides Gallimard

Le Chemin de Saint-Jacques en Espagne

De Saint-Jean-Pied-de-Port à Compostelle – Camino Frances
Jean-Yves Grégoire – Louis Laborde-Balen

Carnets de Saint-Jacques de Compostelle

François Dermaut – Glénat

Collection Miam Miam Dodo – Sur le GR 65 – Du Puy-en-Velay à Saint-Jean-de-Pied-de-Port

Lauriane Clouteau – Jacques Clouteau
Les Editions du Vieux Crayon

Association de Coopération Interrégionale – Les Chemins de Saint-Jacques de Compostelle

La voie du Puy-en-Velay

Printed in the United States
By Bookmasters